Conspiracy Theories in Turkey

Conspiracy theories are no longer just a curiosity for aficionados but a politically salient theme in the age of Trump, Brexit and "fake news". One of the countries that has been entrapped in conspiratorial visions is Turkey, and this book is the first comprehensive survey in English of the Turkish conspiratorial mind-set.

It provides a nuanced overview of the discourses of Turkish conspiracy theorists and examines how these theorists argue for and legitimize their worldview. The author discusses a broad range of conspiracy theories, including some influenced by Kemalist and Islamist perspectives as well as those of the ruling Justice and Development Party. The most influential authors, books, references and images within the conspiracist milieu are all examined in detail.

This book will be an important source for scholars interested in extremism in Turkey and the societal and political impact of conspiracy theories.

Dr. Doğan Gürpınar is based at Istanbul Technical University, Turkey.

T0347735

Conspiracy Theories

Series Editors: Peter Knight, *University of Manchester*, and Michael Butter, *University of Tübingen*.

Conspiracy theories have a long history and exist in all modern societies. However, their visibility and significance are increasing today. Conspiracy theories can no longer be simply dismissed as the product of a pathological mind-set located on the political margins.

This series provides a nuanced and scholarly approach to this most contentious of subjects. It draws on a range of disciplinary perspectives including political science, sociology, history, media and cultural studies, area studies and behavioural sciences. Issues covered include the psychology of conspiracy theories, changes in conspiratorial thinking over time, the role of the Internet, regional and political variations and the social and political impact of conspiracy theories.

The series will include edited collections, single-authored monographs and short-form books.

Impossible Knowledge
Conspiracy Theories, Power, and Truth
Todor Hristov Dechev

The Stigmatization of Conspiracy Theory since the 1950s
"A Plot to Make us Look Foolish"
Katharina Thalmann

Conspiracy Theories in Turkey
Conspiracy Nation
Doğan Gürpınar

Conspiracy Theories in Turkey

Conspiracy Nation

Doğan Gürpınar

Routledge
Taylor & Francis Group

LONDON AND NEW YORK

First published 2020
by Routledge
2 Park Square, Milton Park, Abingdon, Oxon OX14 4RN

and by Routledge
605 Third Avenue, New York, NY 10017

First issued in paperback 2020

*Routledge is an imprint of the Taylor & Francis Group,
an informa business*

British Library Cataloguing-in-Publication Data
A catalogue record for this book is available from the British Library

Library of Congress Cataloging-in-Publication Data
A catalog record for this book has been requested

ISBN 13: 978-0-367-72770-3 (pbk)
ISBN 13: 978-0-367-03093-3 (hbk)

Typeset in Times New Roman
by Apex CoVantage, LLC

Contents

Figures

Acknowledgements

I am intellectually deeply indebted to İlkan Dalkuç as his many points, suggestions and caveats have significantly improved the text. I would also like to thank Pınar Sağlav for taking the time to read parts of the work and for her helpful comments. Colin Sutcliffe thoroughly proofread the text, and Rebecca McPhee meticulously prepared the text for production. I also benefited from the insights of European Union COST Action on Conspiracy Theories (CA15101 or Comparative Analysis of Conspiracy Theories abbreviated as COMPACT) group as a collectivity. I thank them all for their inputs. Finally, I am deeply grateful to series editors Peter Knight and Michael Butter who initiated and led the five-year project. Their interest in my project made it possible for this book to come out.

Introduction

Until two decades ago, when the first cohort of conspiracy study scholars, including Peter Knight, Timothy Melley and Mark Fenster, among others, delved into the field, conspiracy theories were treated as eccentricities not well suited for serious academic study,[1] being seen as a distraction from the sober political, social and ideological mainstays that social sciences were expected to investigate and elaborate on. It was also no coincidence that the first conspiracy theory scholars came exclusively from the academic field of American studies, in that conspiracy theories were conceived of at the time as an idiosyncrasy of the American cultural field. This was before conspiracy theories became a global fascination and threat.

Conspiracy theories were long seen as belonging exclusively to the "fringe" and the extreme right, safely remote from the mainstream and a part of the political spectrum that was seen to have been effectively excluded from the legitimate political space since the end of World War II. Yet, a decade after Francis Fukuyama heralded and celebrated the end of ideologies on the eve of the imminent peaceful and liberal post–Cold War order, the void left behind by the once-popular ideologies with mass appeal was filled by conspiratorial thinking as ersatz ideology. Although for a decade this drift was overlooked and regarded as the last stand of the fringe against neoliberal rationalism, with the dawning of the age of populism, Donald Trump, Brexit and the resurgence of the continental far right, conspiracy theories became the mainstream, having been personified in Donald Trump and sealing the fate of a country, as in the Brexit referendum in 2016.[2] By the 2000s, a new generation of conspiracy theory scholars, who, rather than treating them as insane ramblings, saw them an innate human propensity that needed to be dispassionately studied had begun to speak of "depathologizing conspiracy theories".[3] Conspiracy theories themselves may be hollow and absurd, but the fact that a sizable proportion of the public, including the well-educated, believe them, makes them a salient subject for rigorous academic study.

Turkey also experienced a "conspiratorial turn". Although Turkey's infatuation with conspiracy theories cannot be said to have begun under the incumbent Islamist government headed by Recep Tayyip Erdoğan, it was certainly carried to new heights by President Erdoğan, who bombastically exploits conspiratorial themes to defame/demonize his opponents and to mold a narrative that delineates two irreconcilable camps. Erdoğan's image and his proneness for conspiracy theories have been an object of ridicule both at home and abroad. This study, however, rather than treating conspiracy theories as an eccentricity and folly, contextualizes the recent rise of conspiratorial rhetoric in Turkey at both a state and a popular level. Rather than focusing specifically on the recent conspiratorial turn, this study posits it within a historical trajectory.

This study further attempts to contextualize the Turkish conspiratorial universe in a historical and structural setting rather than attributing it to certain cultural propensities. In many regards, Turkish conspiracy theories replicated the Counter-Enlightenment conspiracy theories followed by the trend-setting Protocols of Elders of Zion account amid the imperial retreat and the fear of national obliteration that burgeoned in the late 19th century. That said, they also carry authentic characteristics of the imported master narrative, benefiting from the emotive and ideational reservoir of Turkish nationalism in which the anti-Masonic Counter-Enlightenment conspiracy theories and the Elders of Zion plot, among others, were appropriated and aromatized in line with local tastes.

The national master narrative was derived from the fear of national annihilation by the imminent threats from abroad (in the age of the empire) and within. This fear and perceived extreme vulnerability and exposure brought about not only a nationalist furor but also a conspiratorial mind-set that saw enemies everywhere against whom one should be ever watchful. Although the master narrative was first propagated by the Young Turks and inherited by the Kemalists, the Islamist master narrative rose out of the same conjecture. The birth of conspiracy theories related to Jews and Freemasons can be dated to the early 20th century and benefited from the Zionist demands to settle in the then–Ottoman territory of Palestine and the idiosyncratic community of Dönme (conversos). The association and even equating of Young Turks, and then Kemalists, with the Freemasonry and Zionists, formed the basis of Islamist conspiracy theories.

Hence, the conspiratorial vision in Turkey was very much entrenched in the discursive formations of the national narrative that was inculcated in the late 19th century and then mastered in the early 20th century. Yet while the nation-statist narrative could command consensus over society in its prime states, in the age of diversity and pluralism and the demise of the capacity of nation-states to impose monolithic political and cultural identities and norms by the late 20th century, this paradigm ceased to wield consensus. As a result, conspiracy theories became conducive at a time of crisis when the now increasingly anachronic national master narrative needed to respond to and counter new developments and discourses (the rise of identity politics, globalization, erosion of the national identity). The fragments and themes of the national narrative were appropriated to arrive at a conspiratorial updated version of the narrative.

This political and cultural drift is a global trend that is ubiquitous in the early 21st century. While in Turkey the rise of conspiracy theories was partially a sequel to the global conspiratorial turn, it also stemmed partially from the Turkish national discursive space entrenched in its historicity. This study examines the Turkish conspiratorial mind, and throughout the book, I seek to delineate the mental continuum of this conspiratorial universe through the 20th century. The first chapter delineates the Turkish master narrative that was established in the early 20th century that still holds sway, while the second chapter delves into the Islamist counternarrative that duplicates, in part, the master narrative but partially overturns and challenges its chief premises. After providing this historical background, the third chapter examines the neo-Kemalist conspiracy theories in the age of conspiracy theories (2000s and beyond), while the final chapter focuses on the Islamist conspiracy theories both as an ideational set and as a means of governance.

Notes

1 For the American right-wing conspiracy theory industry, see Peter Knight, *Conspiracy Culture: American Paranoia from Kennedy to the 'X-Files'* (New York: Routledge, 2001); Robert Alan Goldberg, *Enemies Within* (New Haven: Yale University, 2001); Timothy Melley, *Empire of Conspiracy* (Ithaca: Cornell University Press, 2000); Michael Barkun, *A Culture of Conspiracy* (Berkeley: University of California Press, 2003); Mark Fenster, *Conspiracy Theories: Secrecy and Power in American Culture* (Minneapolis: University of Minnesota Press, 1999).
2 For the conspiratorialism of the mounting European populism, see Eirikur Bergmann, *Conspiracy & Populism: The Politics of Misinformation* (Basingstoke: Palgrave Macmillan, 2018).
3 Cas Mudde, the prominent scholar of European extremism and populism defines such right-wing politics as pathological normal rejecting to label them as merely pathological. *Cas Mudde, On Extremism and Democracy in Europe* (London: Routledge, 2016), 9–11.

1 The Turkish conspiratorial setting

The national narrative

This chapter provides an outline of the underpinnings and the cultural and ideological frames of the Turkish conspiratorial universe and its master narrative. Comparable to other national patterns, Turkish conspiracy theories (CTs) are deeply grounded within a specific historicity and discursive space. Their emergence, dissemination and preponderance are possible only if they comply with preexisting ideas and sentiments. Rather than providing a list of CTs, this chapter presents a brief overview of the making of modern Turkey and the unfolding incipient Turkish nationalist mind. Examining and deliberating on the traumas revolving around the collapse of the Ottoman Empire, the chapter explains the origins and fantasies of Turkish nationalism in pursuit of lost past grandeur under the shadow of the imperial retreat.[1]

This discursive framework is built on the Turkish nationalist metanarrative, the rise of which, like any other incipient nationalist narrative, was based on an array of preconceptions in which Turkishness has been perceived as an organic and fixed entity throughout the course of history. Nations were considered as scientifically proven organic entities with their own lifetimes, rises and falls, with interests that would inevitably clash with others in a zero-sum world entangled within a permanent Darwinian struggle to survive and dominate. Time is merely another dimension in the universe of eternal nations, and the nation is an unchanging entity throughout the course of history against which threats are also perpetual and omnipresent. In the Turkish account, Value-loaded historical references, such as the Crusades, the Holy Alliance and Byzantium, serve to corroborate and affirm these premises, demonstrating the perpetuity of animosities.[2] These preconceptions and fantasies of nationhood lead to a conspiratorial framing of not only current politics but also history, positing historical episodes and themes within the larger conspiratorial setting.

The demise of an empire: the Ottoman legacy

It is a fact that the Ottoman Empire collapsed. This is not a conspiracy theory but a basic truth, yet from the armchair historian's perspective with the hindsight of a century, the causes of its demise seem very different to those propounded by the Young Turks (and later by the Kemalists). The Ottoman Empire epitomized the golden age and the zenith of Turkishness in the eyes of the early generation of Turkish nationalists. This past glory assured its potential, despite the present-day gloom and promised national rejuvenation at a time of national decay. Once militarily invincible, the empire deteriorated for many reasons that were economic, cultural, intellectual and military in nature. The first Turkish nationalists (who were modernists) laid the blame for the present-day backwardness on the self-serving, rotten Ottoman state elite, whom they believed had been corrupted by sycophancy of the court, yet it was not only the Ottomans who were to blame, as other conspirators also contributed to the imperial deterioration. It is also necessary to be aware of all these if one is to understand today and tomorrow, and remain attentive to the enemies that are eternal and perpetual. This national metanarrative that was inculcated in the late 19th century, at a time of imperial decay, was followed by the imperial collapse in a few decades.

This perspective presumed that the Ottoman Empire had been partitioned as a result of the collaboration between the Christian/imperialist powers and the political unreliables within. The nation's foes were thus twofold, being international and domestic: the international foes were (no surprise) the great European powers – first and foremost arch-imperialist Britain (which, in fact, does not corroborate with the historical truth, as it was Russia that posed the greatest threat to the Ottoman Empire), while domestically, the enemies of the nation were the non-Muslims, who were being steered and manipulated by their political and religious leadership; ethnic separationists, including Muslims; and rootless liberal (cosmopolitan) intellectuals who had fallen under the spell of Western propaganda, along with other subversives. All the enemies of the empire were thus amalgamated, tightly associated and rendered as extensions and accomplices of the overarching global plot. Denying them any political and ideological agency, domestic enemies were perceived not only as willing fifth columnists but also as on the payroll of a mastermind.

Unsurprisingly, the non-Muslims, as the usual suspects, were affirmed as the main enemies within the nation's borders, harboring agendas, predispositions and interests that not only complied with but also collectively contradicted the interests of the Ottoman state. The non-Muslims grew rich throughout the 19th century, acting as middlemen between the incoming

European merchants and the local peasantry.[3] Their complicity with the encroaching European capitalism ensued their self-interests diverge from those of the Ottoman state. Their enrichment was evidence of their treachery in the eyes of those who considered the economy to be a zero-sum game, presuming that the non-Muslims should have grabbed the wealth of the Muslims in the first instance.[4] The elusive "cosmopolitans" (*kozmopolitler*) also had a share in the Ottoman retreat, as by being ideologically depraved and unreliable, they were influential in the dissemination of perilous ideas with the potential to weaken and corrupt national awareness and vigilance.

The 19th-century Ottoman reformation (known as the Tanzimat era, initiated in 1839) had sought to create an inclusive political Ottoman community based on civic principles, the assurance of basic rights and liberties and the maintenance of sustainable imperial peace and order.[5] Yet the project failed for many reasons, not only because the Ottoman state and bureaucracy were reluctant to implement the due measures and to grant and expand civil rights but also because no sense of affinity could be forged between the two parties. The more rights given or conceded, the more rights the non-Muslims demanded.[6] This was both a perception and a reality and couldn't be otherwise unless a sense of Ottoman common super-identity could be spawned.[7] It was, however, beyond the reach of the insufficiently flexible Ottoman state elite to engender an Ottoman political community and a political contract.

The empire thus became a battleground for a number of militarized separationist movements, including the Armenians in Eastern Anatolia and the Bulgarians in Macedonia. Abdülhamid II (r. 1876–1909) opted to abandon the relatively lenient policies of his reformist predecessors and to apply brazen iron-fisted policies that crushed the Armenian insurgency but failed gravely in Macedonia.[8] The distrust between the non-Muslim communities and the ruling elite could not be overcome and had become insurmountable by the late 19th century, while the troubles in Macedonia grew as the Ottoman gendarmerie failed to respond effectively to the notorious and violent Bulgarian rebels (known as the *committadji*) who had taken effective control of the Macedonian countryside. This they had achieved despite being countered also by Greek and Serbian groups who were voicing their own claims on Macedonia based on their ethnic presence in the region. In short, the Ottoman state failed to wield authority over its sovereign territories. The sultan Abdülhamid II not only ruled the empire with an iron fist but also introduced a pervasive culture of conspiracy. Suspecting subversion at every instance, he designed a surveillance state obsessed with collecting information by informants within the empire and by embassies abroad, further feeding his mistrust.[9] Hamidian culture of conspiracy was inherited and appropriated by Young Turks who had dethroned the sultan.

As the unruly Macedonia continued to be a crucible of sedition, the brightest young cadets, upon graduation from the Ottoman Military Academy, were sent to the Third Army based in Salonica to fight and subdue the Bulgarian militancy. These officers on duty nurtured a love/hate relationship with their nemeses, being spellbound by the brutal efficiency and discipline of the Bulgarian guerillas and their self-taught erudition, patriotism, selflessness, commitment and readiness to sacrifice themselves for their nation.[10] As the Ottoman state continued failing in its efforts to establish order and governance, the Russian czar Nicholas II and the British king Edward VII met in Reval (Tallinn) and agreed to launch and international intervention. This move unnerved young Ottoman cadets who subsequently rebelled against Sultan Abdülhamid II to upend the otherwise imminent Ottoman retreat from the Balkan lands. The young officers had long been critical of the sultan for the enduring miserable state of the empire, believing that it was his lack of capacity, resolve and patriotic commitment, as well as those of his cronies – the octogenarian pashas with no modern education, who were in complete contrast to the well-trained young officers from the military academy and their Prussian instructors – who were responsible for this humiliation. They further believed that once the cohort of young officers took over the Ottoman state, they would restore order, deliver efficient governance and assure military prowess.

One recurrent contention among the Young Turks in opposition revolved around the possibility of cooperation with non-Muslim dissidents against Abdülhamid II, while a second intra-debate involved the acceptability of any possible collusion with the European powers to overthrow the despised sultan. In a congress convened in Paris in 1902, the flamboyant Prince Sabahaddin advocated cooperation with the Armenian Dashnaks, who were demanding autonomy and expansion of civil rights rather than independence, as the Armenians were not in the majority over any sizeable territory. Yet Sabahaddin's efforts remained marginal and ineffective; as for the overwhelming majority of the Young Turks, the anti-sultanic dissent was an intra-Turkish matter, and such proposals were dismissed outright.[11]

The early Young Turks pursued neither an ethnic agenda nor priorities, and many of the Young Turks were not actually ethnic Turks, coming from Albanian, Kurdish or Circassian backgrounds. Yet, regardless of their ethnic identity, they perceived the survival of the imperial center and its continuation as intact and firmly centralized as the only possible alternative to total destruction and doom for their well-being as any alternative would ensure Christian preponderance. For these reasons, the endurance of the dynasty was imperative for them, not because they were monarchists but because no other scenario could secure and sustain their preponderance. They thus became intransigent champions of the increasingly Turkified, centralized and discriminatory empire.[12] This was a modern nationalized empire, having transformed from a premodern one in which ethnic loyalties were deemed irrelevant as long as political loyalty was assured, into one in which ethnic loyalties mattered, given the failure of the empire to generate other, more solid allegiances.[13]

For these reasons, after Abdülhamid II's deposition, following a swansong of Ottomanism laden for a few months with romantic appeal and optimism, the Young Turks in power drifted toward radical Turkist and authoritarian policies, despite their hitherto rhetoric of rights, liberties and freedom.[14] For the Young Turks, it was crystal clear that non-Muslims were only heinously exploiting the rights and liberties rhetoric while deviously pursuing agendas that were in diametric opposition to the interests of the imperial center and the gullible Turks. It was only ethnic Turks whose self-interests coalesced with those of the imperial center, as all the other ethnic groups sought to look after their own interests in a prospective imperial collapse, and this would bring the national obliteration of Turks, who would be defenseless at the hands of avenging enemies. For this reason, the Young Turks' gravitation toward Turkish nationalism could be considered as being based on the incompatibility of the priorities, concerns and allegiances of the imperial center with those of non–Turkish Ottoman ethnic groups.[15] Only the Turks had sufficient reason to maintain allegiance to the imperial center, which resulted in severe mistrust and resentment towards the non-Turkish communities, who were considered no less than traitors and therefore deserving of their fate.

The Young Turks also had good reason not to trust the European powers. Britain was mistrustful of the Young Turks, seeing them as the henchmen of the Germans, and had long perceived the Ottoman Empire to be a power on the verge of collapse, resulting in a reluctance to invest. The British, rather, sought to increase their military buildup, first, to counter the impending Russian advancement and, later, to "contain German restlessness"[16] on the southern tier of the Ottoman Empire, from the Persian Gulf to Egypt. The imperialist European powers were already preparing for the imminent dissolution of the Ottoman Empire. Italy seized Ottoman Libya, joining the scramble for Africa, while Egypt had already been occupied by the British since 1882. For the Young Turks the picture was crystal clear. European capital had always been fully integrated and freely exchanged across the Ottoman territories, running banks, railways and facilities and buying cheap raw materials and selling industrial goods, killing local proto-industry and artisanship. The Ottoman lands would eventually surrender to the clutches of imperialism unless countered by an effective military resolve.

Amid such a geopolitical quagmire and legitimization crisis in the Ottoman Empire, it did not take long for the Young Turks to come up with a scheme that amalgamated all the "enemies" that they should overwhelm. Their evolving ideological buildup presumed a far-reaching showdown between "us" and "them", the two categories being natural, inherent,

Figure 1.1 Turkish refugees fleeing their ancestral lands traumatizing the retreating nation facing "national annihilation".

Source: Wikimedia

impermeable, absolute and prevailing, fixed in time through the centuries. Şevket Süreyya Aydemir (1897–1976), in his memoirs, reflected on his youthful passions in the 1910s:

> In all the harangues [we heard], the never-ending rebellions were spoken of as passing and minor phenomena, and merely the exploits of those bought by the foreign powers with money. It was said that the real perpetrators were different. There were in fact two clashing forces: the Ottoman Empire on the one side and the Great Powers on the other (the *Düvel-i Muazzama*, composed of the six European great powers, as if their interests were fully coinciding).[17]

As good social Darwinists, the Young Turks also considered national life to be an arena of perpetual war that was in need of strict regulation and order.[18] For them, war was not merely a military involvement pursued at the fronts but also a lifetime encounter that was fought in times of both war and peace on different fronts, beginning with the training of preschool children.[19] Trusting no one, they included among their enemies not only the foreign powers who were openly invoking their conceited ambitions over the Ottoman territory but also those with sinister agendas within the nation's borders. Conspiracy was omnipresent and omnipotent, meaning that a patriot had to be constantly vigilant.

The "cosmopolitan" intellectuals were also seen to be complicit, inadvertently serving the grand plot, and were caricaturized as naïve ignoramuses with no grasp of actual politics, incapable of gauging the real intentions of the ominous European powers that had easily duped them. This was demonstrated most succinctly in the stories of Ömer Seyfeddin (1884–1920), the notable nationalist literary intellectual of the time:

> His religion was Cosmopolitanism. He obstinately worshipped the fixation of the idle, dreadful and pathological thinkers . . . in delusion out of touch with the real world . . . As a resolute and dogmatic Freemason he knew no truth beyond Freemasonry. He accepted neither tradition, history, country nor nation. He renounced the theories of race as those who are mentally and morally sick . . . The concepts of virtue and cosmopolitanism wrecked his intellect and turned him into a living corpse.[20]

Although the CTs vary in content and style, their underlying thrust was fixed, being partially improvised over the European ur-CTs: the Protocols of the Elders of Zion and earlier theories from which this conspiracy had been adapted, beginning with the anti-Illuminati craze and the thriving conspiracies implicating the French Revolution.[21] These CTs all painted a picture of an impeccable cabal of dark forces who were hell-bent on domineering and manipulating the lesser actors, and who were committed to destroying "us", whoever the "us" may refer to. This account conceived two inherently antagonistic camps with contradictory interests that would lead them to an inevitable clash. Although the structure was left intact, the substance was appropriated, localized and nationalized.

Sèvres versus Lausanne

The Turkish national anthem, which is still sung before national football matches as a demonstration of pride and national euphoria, as well as during official ceremonies and other occasions, was written back in 1921 at a time when the Greek army was not far from Ankara, as the seat of Parliament. The anthem begins "Fear not!", assuring the beholder that "the crimson flag will not . . . fade until the last hearth in the nation burns out", capturing and monumentalizing the gloomy and pessimistic state of mind that was ubiquitous at a time when the survival of the nation was at stake. This was a time when nations could be wiped out as political bodies, as the disappearance of the once-mighty Polish nation was a haunting and Cassandran reminder ("Poland has not yet Perished" as the to-be Polish national anthem cried throughout the 19th century)[22] for many.[23] The annihilation of

Armenians was a recent memory, as the perpetrators knew well who had struck preemptively to escape their own otherwise impending doom.

The anthem's reiteration and regularization of these shivering verses, however, resulted in the eternalization, naturalization and normalization of the existential fear of national doom and annihilation as the order of the day. The sentiment would later be dubbed "Sèvres Syndrome" after the Treaty of Sèvres that was signed in 1920 between the victorious allies and the defeated Ottoman Empire (but not recognized by the National Movement based in Ankara) less than a year before the anthem was written. The clauses of the treaty were devastating for the Ottoman Party, requiring it to dissolve most of its military and relinquish significant territory, including Turkish-majority areas. Eastern Thrace and the environs of Izmir (Smyrna) were to be ceded to Greece, based on a (likely to be a rigged) plebiscite, and an Armenian state was also to be founded in the east, with a probable Kurdistan to be decided on later, which would confine the Turkish populace to inner Anatolia.

Sèvres was overturned thanks to the military genius and audaciousness of Mustafa Kemal (Atatürk), who reorganized and assumed the command of the rump Ottoman army. Upon his military victory, the treaty was rescinded and renegotiated, introducing favorable clauses to the Turkish party in the Treaty of Lausanne signed in 1923 that annulled the former Treaty of Sèvres. Since then, in Turkish political discourse, however, Sèvres and Lausanne imply so much more than two treaties. The term *Sèvresphobia* was coined in the 1990s to expound the unyielding belief that Turkey was under imminent attack from the West in a bid to overturn the Treaty of Lausanne.[24]

This paradigm established a mutually exclusive dichotomy between the two treaties. While Lausanne epitomized the deliverance from the throes of imperialism that had been imposed over the Ottoman Empire for at least a century, Sèvres, in contrast, was seen as the very quintessence of the mischievous ends sought and attained by the West, as a metaphysical entity. Sèvres implied subjugation to the Western imperialist enemies not only in political but also ideological terms, smacking of empty imperial pageantry, sycophancy, effeminacy, a servile culture, the self-serving Ottoman *ancien régime* and cosmopolitan liberals. Lausanne, in contrast, denoted selfless zeal, commitment, masculinity, audaciousness and resolve, along with ideological self-righteousness.[25] The Treaty of Lausanne, signed just three months before the proclamation of the republic, was regarded as sacrosanct by secular nationalists in that it resulted in the establishment of the secular republic and the liberation of Anatolia from European and Greek occupation (and imperialism),[26] the two being inseparable; for them, there could be no secular republic without Lausanne!

The scheme also offered "history in a nutshell", making a definite and compact interpretation of the course of modern Turkish history. In brief, this meta-narrative posited the Sèvres and Lausanne treaties as two antagonistic, decisive moments in modern Turkish history[27] and suggested that the Western powers had never renounced their claims or longing for Sèvres. Westerners never forget or learn (or forgive), like the Bourbons, but only changed the means by which they conspired, switching to subtler schemes that were more difficult to fathom unless the beholder was adequately equipped to spot such conspiracies. To these ends, they have since then supported and sponsored the subversive forces within Turkey, especially the Kurdish separatism and Islamic movements that aimed to weaken the Kemalist republican ethos.[28] On top of all these, Sharif Hussein's rebellion during WWI helped and partially organized by T. E. Lawrence, further boosted this scare and fostered a stab-in-the-back myth immortalizing the Arab treachery against the caliph. This episode was instrumental in the Kemalist framing depicting Arabs as willing accomplices of imperialism who were zealously and delusively favored and praised by Turkish conservatives as their Muslim brethren and nation of the prophet. This delusion was shown as an evidence of Turkish Islamists' ideological fixation and foolhardiness. Armenian genocide was also justified on the grounds of Armenians being in the service of imperialist powers. These discourses stemmed from the dread of national annihilation and imperial doom.[29]

The Manichean and conspiratorial iconography also served well in the dissemination and perpetuation of this fear. Although the treaty signed between Turkey and the victors envisaged only a portion of Anatolian territory being ceded, the tripartite agreement signed between the victors on the very same day delineated zones of influence encompassing the Mediterranean and Aegean coasts, as well as larger chunks of Anatolia, in which the "special interests" of France and Italy were recognized. The zones of influence, however, were later inscribed into the national memory as territorial cessations confining Turks to the aridness of inner Anatolia. Conflating the political and economic carvings of Anatolia, this map had become an acute visualization of the treachery faced by the nation, brazenly exposed in one (manipulative) map, and has since become a household image that every Turkish student encounters in the classroom, in textbooks and, later in life, in the media and elsewhere. This map, first published by the Turkish General Staff in 1928 (see Figure 1.2) and replicated ever since, also inscribed the projected US mandate of Armenia in the aftermath of World War I that was not pursued. Although the General Staff map explained the markings in the caption, the map was reproduced exponentially without explanatory captions. Although there are clauses in the Sèvres Treaty pertaining to possible transfer of territory to Armenia (articles 89–90–91) to be settled later arbitrated by the United States (without any certain territorial delineation), this map obscures such uncertainties.

The conflation of all rendered them as part of Sèvres deal in the national mind. This imagery clearly depicted the innate incompatibility of the two discursive universes: one being republican, idealist, patriotic and selfless,

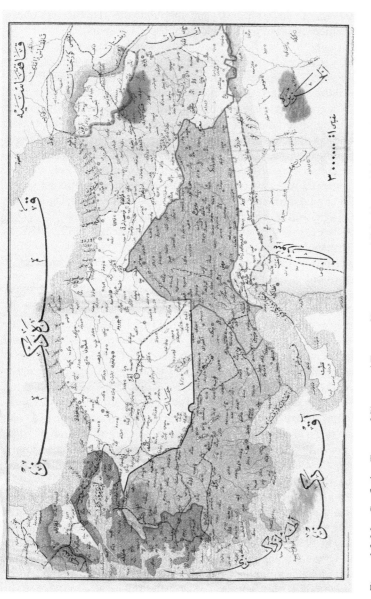

Figure 1.2 Map Conflating Treaty of Sèvres and Treaty of Lausanne as published by Turkish General Staff in 1928.

Source: Supplement of *Derin Tarih* (2015), Private Collection of Mustafa Armağan

and the other selfish, unpatriotic and impervious to the social woes. This narrative will be further reinvigorated relating the post-1980 neoliberal and postnational order to Sèvres mindset and upholding the Kemalist republican thrust in turbulent times to the unyielding spirit of Lausanne.

With Lausanne, the territories lost in the World War I were formally bequeathed, yet the magnitude of the land that remained in Turkish hands was pleasing when compared to the size of the Turkish population vis-à-vis the "rivalling" nations. Much more important, the republic was fully Turkified by means a massacre, population exchange and intimidation in the 15 years leading up to Lausanne. This homogenization also provided relief to the republican elite, allowing them to remain unfettered by any Western imperialist pretext of interference.[30] The treaty brought about an emancipation from imperialist bondage, and thanks to the peace secured in Lausanne, the young republic was able to pursue an intransigently isolationist policy in the 1920s at a time when all of the European powers were trying to overcome war fatigue and reverse their military frailty.

The anti-Westernist ethos of the Kemalist regime abated in the 1930s as Hitlerite Germany and, more significantly for Turkey, fascist Italy, with its impending claims in the eastern Mediterranean, rose as expansionist threats.[31] Gravitating toward the status quo powers of Britain and France, Turkey pursued an "active neutrality" during World War II, vying to balance the German and Russian aggressions.[32] After the war ended with the utter victory of the Allies, Turkey continued to side with Britain and the United States against the invigorated Russian threat. As democracy became the order of the day and authoritarianism was discredited under the boots of the US soldiers, the Turkish political culture also transformed. Twisting the Kemalist justification for autocracy, it was now argued that after two decades of "tutelage" on the road to full democracy, Turkey was now ready for it. The Kemalist era was retrospectively reinterpreted as a transitory period for democracy, simultaneously justifying authoritarian rule and reconciling it with the impending democratization.[33]

Turkey not only moved toward a multiparty democracy but also joined the transatlantic alliance, alarmed by the swelling Soviet threat from the north. This was a policy that was initiated by İsmet İnönü (1874–1973, president of Turkey, 1938–1950) and furthered by Menderes, as the first democratically elected prime minister, bringing about an end to Kemalist rule in 1950.[34] Turkey became a member of North Atlantic Treaty Organization (NATO) in 1952, as, while the Kemalist regime had pursued a firm isolationist policy and maintained close relations with the Soviet Union, this was no longer tenable amid the Cold War entanglements and alignments.[35]

This foreign policy shift unnerved mistrustful minds. For many this was clear and brazen proof of a selling-out of the Kemalist stand against encroaching imperialism. Yet two views clashed with regard to the dating and specifics. For some, the sell-out was a ploy of the Democrat Party, who they accused of market liberalism, pro-Americanism and of sympathizing and conceding to Islamic reaction, while for others, the sell-out had begun at the death bed of Atatürk in 1938. Unable to match the charisma, political aptitude and ideological faultlessness of Atatürk, İnönü was charged for succumbing to the Western powers and abandoning the Kemalist nationalism, stature and valor. The anti-İnönü paradigm contrasted Atatürk's and İnönü's lines. Whereas the former was an incarnation of the national bulwark and the safeguarding of full sovereignty, the latter was an ill-advised Westernophile who misunderstood and distorted Atatürk's cultural revolution and diluted and made effeminate the national self by succumbing subserviently to Western culture.[36]

For the Turkish secular-nationalist conspiratorial universe, the national idea is robustly and inextricably ingrained within the very self of Atatürk. Any diversion from his principles is tantamount to national treason. Furthermore, it is unimaginable that anyone would ever willingly renounce and dismiss national belonging. Anyone who deviates from this sublime republican ideal could only be construed as accomplices to the global master conspiracy or commanded and readily manipulated by a puppet master, namely the United States.

From Kemalism to socialism (1950–1990)

Kemalism conceived two irreconcilable camps: the camp of reaction versus the camp of progressivism. Kemalist progressivism was resolutely nationalist, firmly upholding national vigor and ethos, and bearer of the project of national enlightenment. As an ideology, it blended nationalism and faith in modernity, perceiving modernization as a transformative agent of the nation. This conviction was almost unequivocally endorsed by the intellectuals, although the Kemalist-nationalist consensus gradually eroded as the new generation of intellectuals started to move toward the left. Yet these two predispositions were not necessarily mutually exclusive, and many of these intellectuals subscribed to a socialist modernity project in which the state would be expected to uphold progressive values and to bring about social and cultural transformation, ingrained with progressive ethos and creed. In the second half of the 1940s in particular, at a time when socialism was attaining increasingly high prestige following the Red Army's extermination of the Nazis and "liberation" of Eastern Europe, the intellectuals reappropriated their Kemalist affinities and gradually shifted leftward.[37] This necessitated adjustments and mutations to the Kemalist premises, although a more drastic appropriation came in the 1960s with the adaption of Third-Worldist left nationalism. This blend and twist were dubbed "neo-Kemalism". It challenged and repudiated the status quo Kemalism that was strictly pro-US and Cold War inclined for being "wardrobe Kemalism".[38] The 1960s' Cold War conjuncture was to be historicized and posited within a historical scheme nationalizing the Marxist rendering of history and global order.[39]

This historical account claimed that the Tanzimat reforms had brought about a semicolonization of the Ottoman Empire. The liberal reformism of the Tanzimat era was doomed to fail and collapse, as do all such naïve efforts in that direction. For the Young Turks, and subsequently the Kemalists, Islamists, nationalists and socialists, the Tanzimat elite and "mentality" smacked of cosmopolitanism, liberalism and acquiescence to Western intrusions. This framing was appropriated by the neo-Kemalists of the 1960s, who amalgamated it with Marxism in the Third-Worldist mold. Reading French Marxists at the time of decolonization, the Tanzimat's capitulation to the West (Concert of Europe, imperialist encroachment, liberal reforms) was equated with subservience to US imperialism.

İlhan Selçuk (1925–2010), a charismatic and widely popular socialist and left-Kemalist intellectual who had broad influence over the youth in the 1960s, was preeminent in the molding of a historical vision blending Kemalist and socialist proclivities. His political project was to launch an intellectual second National Struggle against "bogus Atatürkism" and to demolish the reigning "Second Tanzimat". As Kemalism compromised and tempered its ideological buildup and stance toward the Tanzimat and incorporated the Anglo-American anticommunist transnationalism, the socialist youth revolted against the Cold War Kemalism that had made peace with the West. In a highly popular article, he associated Cold War Atatürkists with Tanzimat "dandyism":

> They are no different to the a la franga *beys of the Tanzimat, donning fez, gold spectacles* [. . .] *starched shirts* [. . .] *They are imbecilic dandies who could not comprehend the meaning of the age of Atatürk* [. . .] *They stabbed Atatürk in the back at the first opportunity and compromised with the enemies of Atatürk for a few pennies* [. . .] *Being the foremost servants of this regime, these compradors became the backers [advocates] of the traitors, racketeers, money lenders and agents [of the imperialist powers]* . . . *We have to rescue Atatürkism from these dandy Ottomans who have no clue what Atatürkism is.*[40]

The most comprehensive and erudite articulation of neo-Kemalism formulated and reigned in the 1960s was propounded by Doğan Avcıoğlu (1926–1983), a leading and prolific ideologue of the Kemalist left who amalgamated his Kemalist and socialist commitments. His major work, the two-volume *Türkiye'nin Düzeni* (*The Order of Turkey: Past, Present and Future*),[41] published in 1968 (a work which can legitimately be dubbed as the Turkish *Das Kapital* in terms of its sophistication in theory, historical and social grasp and impact) determined the contours of the neo-Kemalist historiography, benefiting from his Marxist and French readings.

Avcıoğlu placed the Tanzimat at the center of his historical assessment of Turkey and the development of capitalism in the country. Dubbing the Baltalimanı Treaty signed between Britain and the Ottomans in 1838 as "Turkey's death sentence",[42] he sarcastically ridiculed Mustafa Reşid Pasha and the hagiographic historiography sanctioning him, maintaining that "the Great Mustafa Reşid Pasha signed Turkey's death warrant, a document endorsed commencing the unfolding of [modern] Turkey".[43] After lampooning those who called him "great", Avcıoğlu portrayed Mustafa Reşid Pasha as "a paragon of a new type of statesman that emerged with the Tanzimat, who rose up relying on the support of foreign states, reminiscent of the pre-Tanzimat pattern in which future pashas owed their careers to their enrollment in the powerful pashas' retinues/houses". He further noted that as the pre-Tanzimat pashas were domestics of pashas upon their rise to prominence, the master (pasha) of Mustafa Reşid Pasha was the mighty British ambassador Lord Stratford Canning, known as "the sultan of the sultans".[44]

He argued that all the Tanzimat reforms were imposed by Britain to render Turkey a semi-colony and satellite in the disguise of Westernism.[45] For Avcıoğlu, the promulgation of the Edict of Tanzimat in 1839 one year after the Baltalimanı Treaty, and the subsequent Tanzimat culture were merely political and legal superstructure imposed by this economic infrastructure. Juxtaposing the Tanzimat against the anti-imperialist Kemalism, for him the subordination to Western imperialism (which was erroneously dubbed "Westernism") was to be rescinded with the isolationist Kemalist political economy – a pattern that would be later dubbed "delinking" by the neo-Marxist Samir Amin.[46] For Avcıoğlu, the Tanzimat was tantamount to subordination to European imperialism, whereas Atatürk, by severing a Gordian knot, had liberated Turkey from the encroachment of Western imperialism, first militarily and then ideologically. Employing the Marxian methodology and axioms and coalescing them with the Kemalist framework, he contrasted the Tanzimat and Kemalism as two different political economies. This interpretation rendered the Kemalist paradigm more uncompromising and self-righteous.

It was not that Avcıoğlu was crafting a CT. On the contrary, he was an assiduous and well-read intellectual who was well versed in Marxism and history. Yet what Avcıoğlu propounded that Selçuk and others vulgarized was a historical scheme that demonstrated and proved scientifically the viciousness of the elusive West(ern imperialism/capitalism) that was resolutely committed to the elimination of all impediments that could thwart the expansion and domination of (Western/European) capital over the suffering non-Western Third-World peoples. Any political edifices that might oppose this encroachment had to be eradicated or neutralized. European capitalism had colonized Africa and most of Asia and had compromised the sovereignties of countries such as China and Persia, and the Ottoman Empire was just another of its prey. To this end, it had to be politically compromised or neutralized. The Tanzimat and its liberal reformism were sculpted by Britain to this end. Those who countered this Western intrusion and their accomplices (such as Young Turks, nationalist intellectuals, Kemalists, etc.) were, on the other hand, inherently progressive, and their sense of Turkish nationalism was also progressive, standing as a bulwark against imperialist intrusion. They resisted the scheming of the West in the name of national interest and dignity, from which they arrived at anti-imperialism.

It is not difficult to detect the Kemalist coating and nor the pre-Kemalist legacy that survived intact under alternative disguises within this leftist/ Marxist scheme in which no difference between the West, Christendom and global capitalism can be discernible. The elusive *West* serves as a nebulous term that enables the ontologization, essentialization and eternalization of the hostility. This metanarrative supplies the necessary flexibility to allow the nature and underlying motivations behind this elusive West to be spotted. The ambiguity of the term renders its articulation interchangeable, whether referring to Christians, imperialists, capitalists or nation-states (British, French, etc., against the Turks). In this respect, the conspiratorial scheme can easily alter to adapt to Islamist, nationalist (Kemalist) or socialist scripts. The pivot of the Turkish CTs is the sharp and irreconcilable dichotomy that exists between the "West" and "us". This essentialized and eternalized antagonism is shared in the leftist, rightist, Islamist or Kemalist conspiratorial minds.

The rising Third-Worldist and Maoist currents and Marxist imperialism scheme were built on and well suited for this inherited national framing. The ruling center-right and conservative political governments, along with their religious affinities, sympathies and their staunch allegiance to NATO, were amalgamated within a Marxist frame. From 1950 onward, center-right politics dominated the Turkish political scene, establishing an almost permanent hegemony, while the center-left Kemalist RPP [Republican People's Party founded by Atatürk in 1923] could enjoy only brief and interrupted spells in government. The preponderance of the Turkish right during the Cold War determined the contours of the scheme that was sketched and promoted by the left that was fraught with Kemalist proclivities.[47] This scheme envisaged an Establishment that acted in thorough coordination. The feudal aghas, village imams and sheiks were seen as being in collusion with the aghas, fat capitalists living lavish lives, politicians on the payroll of the United States and pseudo-intellectuals doggedly espousing the NATO alliance that made up this ruling coalition under the aegis of US imperialism. Reaction serves imperialism as an impeccable progressive-Marxian premise proved by history.

Against this coalition of power there also endured a progressive, and hence, anti-imperialist, axis. The youth, the academia, as an inherently progressive institution, and the socialist and patriotic intellectuals constituted a nationally aware anti-imperialist alliance that was, on the whole, a Marxist scheme adjusted to the inherited nationalist anti-imperialist scheme. This was not a class-against-class confrontation but an antagonism drawn between victimized people (and, hence, nation) under the threat of imperialism/capitalism and its lackeys. The Marxian scheme was not only adapted to the Turkish setting but also filtered through the inherited preconceptions, mental frames and ideological proclivities. Upon this narrative, the hitherto patriotic youth shifted from Kemalist developmentalism to socialism and socialist developmentalism.

The passing of socialism and the return home

Whereas the 1970s witnessed a rise of socialism, especially among the students, intellectuals and, to a lesser degree, the workers, the military coup of 1980 came down hard on the Turkish left. The junta arrested hundreds of thousands of leftist sympathizers, and tens of thousands were convicted. Torture was ubiquitous. The Turkish leftist organizations and trade unions, along with their networks, were all but eradicated.[48] Although the military coup was a milestone in recent Turkish history, we still know little about its preplanning and the extent of US involvement. The Latin American pattern, in which conservative and hardline anticommunist military regimes were espoused by the United States, is well documented. Pinochet's notorious coup in 1973 haunted the Turkish left, stripping naked the darkest face of US imperialism. Naturally, an analogous nexus was assumed.

The liaisons between US intelligence and the Turkish military were no secret, and the junta's agenda fit well with the priorities of the United States, although the intricacies of the coup are still mostly unknown. For the leftists, however, the US involvement in the junta was beyond doubt.[49] At the time of the coup, in Afghanistan the mujahedeen were being hailed as "freedom fighters" against the godless communists, and as a result, Zbigniew Brzezinski, for a short time, toyed with the idea of launching a "green belt" on the southern tier of the Soviet Union. The Turkish military junta also used Islamic undertones, assuming that a measured consumption of Islam would serve as an antidote to Marxism and a glue for the "national unity", hedging against subversive threats. It was also conducive to its authoritarian agenda, and many suspected this Islamic tinge was actually a US ploy. Accordingly, the conservative politics of the junta were attributed to the deliberate scheming of the United States. Yet for the left and the Kemalists, the US promotion of Islam stemmed not from pragmatic Cold War motivations but from a deliberate and long-term strategy to weaken the acumen and, hence, patriotism of the Turkish people that stemmed from intellectual awareness, rigor and consciousness.[50]

Accordingly, the United States was conceded the right to shape Turkish education through an international agreement signed already by the onset of the Cold War, fully aware of the need to format and brainwash the Turks if it was to be able to undertake its imperialist schemes in the name of Cold War exigencies. The US liaisons and its permanent representatives in the Turkish Ministry of Education under the cover of "advisers" revamped the Turkish education system from the late 1940s (not exonerating İnönü) onward, thus weakening national resolve and intellectual shrewdness.[51] This account cleared the way for the passage from socialism, which opposed US imperialism in the name of global equality and justice, to left-Kemalism, which opposed the United States in the name of national sovereignty and nationalism. Class was gradually substituted by the nation as the fundamental unit that self-styled progressives should uphold in the name of anti-imperialism.

The 1980s heavily tarnished the public prominence and power of the left as a towering social force, and what was worse was the collapse of global socialism as a feasible project with mass appeal by the end of the 1980s. Many disillusioned Turkish socialists abandoned or moderated their leftist commitments and faith in the global revolution for the promise of a better, more progressive and peaceful world guided by Marxist theory, while others sought refuge in reformist and democratic socialism. The new leftist themes gravitated toward anti-militarist, environmentalist, feminist and lesbian, gay, bisexual, and transgender agendas, yet many other disillusioned leftists shunned and even disdained these refugees, claiming that they were tantamount to the wrecking and undoing of socialism. Such shallow fads as homosexuality, the environment and identity were, for them, forsaking the socialist pledge to transform the world and in fact crafted mischievously by the US for this very reason.[52]

Harboring deep hostility to the new left agendas, these disillusioned socialists drifted overwhelmingly toward anti-imperialist Kemalism, keeping their anti-imperialism intact but abandoning their hitherto egalitarian agendas and utopias. In many ways, this was a homecoming and brought about a new ideological amalgamation known in Turkish as *ulusalcılık*. Although the phrase's direct translation into English would be nationalism *per se*, partially because it is a Turkish (Mongolian) word as opposed to the Arabic loanword *milliyetçilik* (the standard word standing for nationalism), it was tinged exclusively with left-leaning, hardline and radically secularist connotations. From their Marxist anti-imperialism, they arrived at a republican nationalism (resembling French *souverainisme*) that represented the main dichotomy between the enlightened and national republic and its enemies in the age of globalization and the demise of nation-states. Obviously, this was only possible thanks to the commonality of the underlying conspiratorial ur-narrative, which I scrutinize in more detail in the third chapter.[53]

Conclusion

This chapter has demonstrated how CTs created an outline of a historical scheme in which the domestic and international enemies of the Kemalist republic had been imagined as not only in collusion but also in close coordination. Domestic enemies such as the Kurdish movement, Islamists and the rootless liberal intellectuals were rendered accomplices to an overarching global plot. The chapter also provided a historical account of the scheme, establishing a historical narrative and continuum that begins in the late Ottoman Empire and culminates in the present. In this, the mainstays of the national metanarrative are delineated, as all ideologies and predispositions were built on this very national ur-narrative that was later appropriated to suit ideological and cultural lines. The following chapter addresses the Islamist counternarrative that was built, in part, on the same thrust and underlying premises but that simultaneously overturned its implications.

Notes

1 For some studies of Turkish conspiracy theories, see Doğan Gürpınar, *Komplolar Kitabı* (İstanbul: Doğan Kitap, 2014); Doğan Gürpınar, *Ulusalcılık: İdeolojik Önderlik ve Takipçileri* (İstanbul: Kitap Yayınları, 2011); Christoph Herzog, "Small and Large Scale Conspiracy Theories and Their Problems: An Example from Turkey", in Maurus Reinkowski, Michael Butter (eds.), *Conspiracy Theories in the United States and the Middle East: A Comparative Approach* (New York: Gruyter, 2014), 139–156; Türkay Nefes, *Online Anti-Semitism in Turkey* (Basingstoke: Palgrave Macmillan, 2015); Marc David Baer, "An Enemy Old and New: The Dönme, Anti-Semitism, and Conspiracy Theories in the Ottoman Empire and the Turkish Republic", *Jewish Quarterly Review*, 103(4), 2013, 523–555; Tanıl Bora, " 'Kitle İmhalarla Yok Etmek Lazım' – Gelişen Anti-Kürt Hınç", *Birikim*, (191), 2005, 36–47; Mesut Yeğen, " 'Yahudi-Kürtler' ya da Türklüğün Yeni Hudutları", *Doğu-Batı*, (29), 2014, 159–178; Doğan Gürpınar, "Historical Revisionism vs. Conspiracy Theories: Transformations of Turkish Historical Scholarship and Conspiracy Theories as a Constitutive Element in Transforming Turkish Nationalism", *Journal of Balkan and Near Eastern Studies*, 15(4), 2013, 1–22; Kerem Karaosmanoğlu, "Türkiye'de Azınlıklar ve Komplo Zihniyeti", *Liberal Düşünce*, 13(50), 2018, 139–158; Kerem Karaosmanoğlu, "Bir Komplo Söyleminden Parçalar: Komplo Zihniyeti, Sıradan Faşizm ve New Age", *Kültür ve İletişim*, 12(1), 2009, 95–126; Necmi Erdoğan, " 'Kalpaksız Kuvvacılar': Kemalist Sivil Toplum Kuruluşları", in Stefanos Yerasimos (ed.), *Türkiye'de Sivil Toplum ve Milliyetçilik* (İstanbul: İletişim Yayınları, 2001), 235–263; Aylin Özman, Kadir Dede, "Türk Sağı ve Masonluğun Söylemsel İnşası: İktidar, Bilinmezlik, Komplo", in İnci Kerestecioğlu, Güven Gürkan Öztan (eds.), *Türk Sağı: Mitler, Fetişler, Düşman İmgeleri* (İstanbul: İletişim Yayınları, 2012), 169–201.

2 For the late 19th-century and early 20th-century employment of historical themes in the service of the nation-in-making, see Doğan Gürpınar, *Ottoman/Turkish Visions of the Nation, 1860–1950* (Basingstoke: Palgrave Macmillan, 2013).

3 For the economics of the transformation, see Reşat Kasaba, *The Ottoman Empire and the World Economy: The Nineteenth Century* (Albany: State University of New York Press, 1988).

4 For such perspectives, see Hilmar Kaiser, *Imperialism, Racism, and Development Theories: The Construction of a Dominant Paradigm on Ottoman Armenians* (London: Gomidas Institute, 1997); Stefan Ihrig, *Justifying Genocide: Germans and the Armenians from Bismarck to Hitler* (Cambridge, MA: Harvard University Press, 2016), 74–79.

5 For the Tanzimat era, see Carter Findley, "The Tanzimat", in Reşat Kasaba (ed.), *The Cambridge History of Turkey* (Cambridge: Cambridge University Press, 2008), v. IV, 11–37.

6 For a truthful account of this dynamic in the breakthrough piece originally published in 1904, see Yusuf Akçura, *Üç Tarz-ı Siyaset* (Ankara: Türk Tarih Kurumu Yayınları, 1976), 28.

7 For the Kemalist and Young Turk narratives of the Tanzimat and the non-Muslim ascendancy in the service of European capitalism, see Doğan Gürpınar, *Ottoman/Turkish Visions of the Nation*, 175–190; Asım Karaömerlioğlu, "Helphand-Parvus and His Impact on Turkish Intellectual Life", *Middle Eastern Studies*, 40(6), 2004, 145–165.

8 For the ethnic violence that flourished in the Ottoman lands, see Hans-Lukas Kieser, *Der Verpasste Friede: Mission, Ethnie und Staat in den Ostprovinzen der Türkei, 1839–1938* (Zürich: Chronos Verlag, 2000); İpek Yosmaoğlu, *Blood Ties: Religion, Violence and the Politics of Nationhood in Ottoman Macedonia, 1878–1908* (Ithaca: Cornell University Press, 2013); James J. Reid, *Crisis of the Ottoman Empire: Prelude to Collapse 1839–1878* (Stuttgart: F. Steiner, 2000); Ryan Gingeras, *Sorrowful Shores: Violence, Ethnicity, and the End of the Ottoman Empire, 1912–23* (Oxford: Oxford University Press, 2009); Bedross Der Matossian, *Shattered Dreams of Revolution: From Liberty to Violence in the Late Ottoman Empire* (Stanford: Stanford University Press, 2014).

9 Doğan Gürpınar, *Ottoman Imperial Diplomacy* (London: I. B. Tauris, 2013); İlkay Yılmaz, *Serseri, Anarşist ve Fesadın Peşinde* (İstanbul: Tarih Vakfı Yurt Yayınları, 2014).

10 For the world of the Bulgarian militias, the Ottoman gendarmerie in its pursuit of the Bulgarian militias and the pervasive violence haunting the countryside and cities, see İpek Yosmaoğlu, *Blood Ties*.

11 M. Şükrü Hanioğlu, *Young Turks in Opposition* (Oxford: Oxford University Press, 1995), 173–199.

12 Ibid., 211–212.

13 Howard Eissenstat, "Modernization, Imperial Nationalization, and the Ethnicization of Confessional Identity in the Late Ottoman Empire", in Stefan Berger, Alexei Miller (eds.), *Nationalizing Empires* (Budapest: Open University Press, 2015), 429–460.

14 For the Young Turks in power, see M. Şükrü Hanioğlu, "The Second Constitutional Period, 1908–1918", in Reşat Kasaba (ed.), *The Cambridge History of Turkey* (Cambridge: Cambridge University Press, 2008), v. IV, 62–111.

15 For example, see Erik Jan Zürcher, *The Young Turk Legacy and Nation Building* (London: I. B. Tauris, 2010); Reşat Kayalı, *Arabs and Young Turks: Ottomanism,*

Arabism, and Islamism in the Ottoman Empire, 1908–1918 (Berkeley: University of California Press, 1997).

16 Marian Kent, "Great Britain and the End of the Ottoman Empire 1900–23", in Marian Kent (ed.), *The Great Powers and the End of the Ottoman Empire* (London: Routledge, 1996), 166. Also see, T. G. Otte, *The Foreign Office Mind: The Making of British Foreign Policy, 1865–1914* (New York: Cambridge University Press, 2011), 99.

17 Şevket Süreyya Aydemir, *Suyu Arayan Adam* (İstanbul: Remzi Kitapevi, 1971), 42.

18 Hans-Lukas Kieser, *Vorkämpfer der "Neuen Türkei"* (Zürich: Chronos, 2005); Cemil Aydın, *The Politics of Anti-Westernism in Asia: Visions of World Order in Pan-Islamic and Pan-Asian Thought* (New York: Columbia University Press, 2007); Palmira Brummett, *Image and Imperialism in the Ottoman Revolutionary Press, 1908–1911* (Albany: State University of New York Press, 2000).

19 Gerhard Grüßhaber, *The "German Spirit" in the Ottoman and Turkish Army, 1908–1938* (Oldenbourg: De Gruyter, 2018), 114–129; Mehmet Beşikçi, *The Ottoman Mobilization of Manpower in the First World War* (Leiden: E. J. Brill, 2012), 203–245; Sanem Yamak Ateş, *Asker Evlatlar Yetiştirmek: II. Meşrutiyet Döneminde Beden Terbiyesi, Askeri Talim ve Paramiliter Gençlik Örgütleri* (İstanbul: İletişim Yayınları, 2012).

20 Ömer Seyfeddin, Primo, Türk Çocuğu, in Ömer Seyfeddin, *Bomba* (İstanbul: Rafet Zaimler Kitap Yayınevi, 1962), 53–54.

21 For Counter-Enlightenment CTs, see Graeme Garard, *Counter-Enlightenments* (London: Routledge, 2006), 42–48; Darrin M. McMahon, *Enemies of the Enlightenment: The French Counter-Enlightenment and the Making of Modernity* (Oxford: Oxford University Press, 2001), 57–65. Also see, Zeev Sternhell, *Neither Right nor Left: Fascist Ideology in France* (Berkeley: University of California Press, 1986); Geoffrey Cubitt, *The Jesuit Myth: Conspiracy Theory and Politics in Nineteenth-Century France* (Oxford: Oxford University Press, 1993). It should be remembered that as self-styled progressives, the Young Turks owed much to such "progressive" conspiracy theories as the Jesuit scare that dominated the 19th-century French republicans.

22 For Polish conceptions of nations that rise, fall and are reborn at a time of no-Poland as a political body, see Patrice M. Dabrowski, *Commemorations and the Shaping of Modern Poland* (Bloomington: Indiana University Press, 2004), 224.

23 For the Turkish nationalist Yusuf Akçura's comparison and warning, see François Georgeon, *Aux origens du nationalisme Turc: Yusuf Akçura (1876–1935)* (Paris: Éditions ADPF, 1980), 129. "Turkish-Ottoman society thus became a defective body, composed only of aristocrats, functionaries and peasants, as in the Kingdom of Poland before its partition. While in Poland, the bourgeoisie was only composed of Jews and Germans, in the 19th century Ottoman state the bourgeoisie was made up of Jews, Greeks, Armenians and non-Turkish indigenous elements".

24 For the Sèvres complex, see Wolfango Piccoli, Dietrich Jung, *Turkey at the Crossroads: Ottoman Legacies and a Greater Middle East* (London: Zed Books, 2001), 115–118; Kemal Kirişçi, Gareth Winrow, *The Kurdish Question and Turkey* (London, Portland: Frank Cass, 1997), 184, 193; Philip Robins, *Suits and Uniforms: Turkish Foreign Policy Since the Cold War* (London: Hurst & Company, 2003), 102–104; Michelangelo Guida, "The Sèvres Syndrome and 'Komplo' Theories in the Islamist and Secular Press", *Turkish Studies*, 9(1), 2008, 37–52; Hakan Yılmaz, "Two Pillars of Nationalist Euroskepticism in Turkey:

The Tanzimat and Sèvres Syndromes", in Ingmar Karlsson, Annika Strom Melin (eds.), *Turkey, Sweden and the European Union: Experiences and Expectations* (Stockholm: Swedish Institute for European Policy Studies, 2006), 29–40.

25 For the establishment of a dichotomy between the republic in Ankara, and the decadent Empire and 19th-century Ottoman reformism (Tanzimat) by the semi-official Kemalist texts, see Yusuf Hikmet Bayur, *Yeni Türkiye Devletinin Harici Siyaseti* (İstanbul: Akşam Matbaası, 1934), 1–3; Yusuf Hikmet Bayur, *Türk Tarihinin Ana Hatları* (İstanbul: Kaynak Yayınları, 1999), 460, 465–466; T. T. T. Cemiyeti, *Tarih III (Yeni ve Yakın Zamanlar)* (Ankara: Devlet Matbaası, 1933), 188–310; Yusuf Hikmet Bayur, *Türk İnkılabı Tarihi* (Türk Ankara: Tarih Kurumu, 1991), v. I, II, 149. Also see, Can Erimtan, *Ottomans Looking West?* (London, New York: I.B. Tauris, 2008), 145–167.

26 For the significance of Lausanne in the ideological and political establishment and the legitimization of the Turkish republic, see Baskın Oran, "1919–1923: Kurtuluş Yılları", in Baskın Oran (ed.), *Türk Dış Politikası* (İstanbul: İletişim Yayınları, 2001), v. I, 222. Temperley, one of the doyens of the history of diplomacy, wrote just one year after the Treaty of Lausanne that this treaty "seemed destined, in all human probability, to inaugurate a more lasting settlement, not only than the Treaty of Sèvres, but than the Treaties of Versailles, St. Germain, Trianon and Neuilly". Temperley's prediction turned out to be impressively accurate. Quoted in M. S. Anderson, *The Eastern Question* (London, Basingstoke: Palgrave Macmillan, 1972), 376.

27 For a comparison of the Treaty of Sèvres and the Treaty of Lausanne, see Baskın Oran, "1919–1923: Kurtuluş Yılları", 237–238.

28 For some examples of the genre relating to 1918 through 1923 to today, see Hulki Cevizoğlu, *İşgal ve Direniş: 1919 ve Bugün* (İstanbul: Ceviz Kabuğu Yayınları, 2007); Hulki Cevizoğlu, *1919'un Şifresi* (İstanbul: Ceviz Kabuğu Yayınları, 2007); Orhan Çekiç, *Mondros'tan İstanbul'a: İmparatorluk'tan Cumhuriyet'e* (İstanbul: Kaynak Yayınları, 2014); Taner Baytok, *İngiliz Belgeleriyle Sevr'den Lozan'a* (İstanbul: Doğan Kitap, 2007). Whereas the subtitle of Cevizoğlu's latter book is "What changed since then?" his former book's title in English is *Occupation and Resistance: 1919 and Today*, establishing a constant continuum from then until now.

29 Lerna Ekmekçioğlu, *Recovering Armenia: The Limits of Belonging in Post-Genocide Turkey* (Stanford: Stanford University Press), 7–8; Hilmar Kaiser, *Imperialism, Racism, and Development Theories: The Construction of a D ominant Paradigm on Ottoman Armenians*, (London: Gomidas Institute, 1997).

30 Bülent Gökay, *A Clash of Empires: Turkey Between Russian Bolshevism and British Imperialism, 1918–1923* (London: I. B. Tauris, 1997), 169.

31 Dilek Barlas, *Etatism and Diplomacy in Turkey* (Leiden: Brill, 1998), 112; Dilek Barlas, *Turkey in the Mediterranean During the Interwar Era* (Bloomington: Indiana University Press, 2010).

32 Selim Deringil, *Turkish Foreign Policy During the World War: An "Active" Neutrality* (Cambridge, New York: Cambridge University Press, 1989).

33 Cemil Koçak, *Belgelerle İktidar ve Serbest Cumhuriyet Fırkası* (İstanbul: İletişim Yayınları, 2006), 633–692.

34 William M. Hale, *Turkish Foreign Policy* (London: Frank Cass, 2000), 111–121; Umut Uzer, *Identity and Turkish Foreign Policy* (London: I. B. Tauris, 2011), 68.

35 John M. Vanderlippe, *The Politics of Turkish Democracy: İsmet İnönü and the Formation of the Multi-Party System, 1938–1950* (Albany: State University of New York Press, 2005), 161–163.

36 Attila İlhan (1925–2005), the eminent Turkish poet, novelist and a socialist intellectual, was the leading proponent of this view. For İlhan, kicked out of high school, imprisoned because of his socialist views during İnönü's presidency and only able to finish high school thanks to his father's connections and efforts, İnönü epitomized capitulation to the West in terms of ideology, culture and economics. This common view among the Kemalist left was also advocated by Berkes (also a victim of İnönü's presidency) and Çetin Yetkin, who also viewed İnönü as retreat from Atatürk's project of national enlightenment. See Attila İlhan, *Hangi Atatürk?* (Ankara: Bilgi Yayınevi, 1981); Attila İlhan, *Hangi Batı?* (Ankara: Bilgi Yayınevi, 1972); Niyazi Berkes, *Unutulan Yıllar* (İstanbul: İletişim Yayınları, 1997); Çetin Yetkin, *Karşıdevrim, 1945–1950* (İstanbul: Otopsi Yayınları, 2003).

37 For glimpses of this mental transformation, see Mete Çetik, *Üniversitede Cadı Kazanı* (İstanbul: İstanbul: Tarih Vakfı Yurt Yayınları, 1998); Niyazi Berkes, *Unutulan Yıllar*; Mustafa Çıkar, *Hasan Âli Yücel* (Ankara: Türkiye İş Bankası Kültür Yayınları, 1997).

38 İlhan Selçuk, "Gardrop Atatürkçülüğü", *Yön*, September 9, 1966.

39 For Turkish neo-Kemalism and the *Yön* (*Direction*) journal and movement headed by Doğan Avcıoğlu, see For the journal *Yön*, see Ergun Aydınoğlu, *Türk Solu (1960–1971)* (İstanbul: Belge Yayınları), 38–46; Igor P. Lipovsky, *The Socialist Movement in Turkey, 1960–1980* (Leiden, New York, Köln: E.J. Brill, 1992), 85–108; Hikmet Özdemir, *Kalkınmada Bir Strateji Arayışı: Yön Hareketi* (Ankara: Bilgi Yayınevi, 1986); Gökhan Atılgan, *Yön-Devrim Hareketi* (İstanbul: TÜSTAV, 2002).

40 İlhan Selçuk, "Gardrop Atatürkçülüğü".

41 Doğan Avcıoğlu, *Türkiye'nin Düzeni* (Ankara: Bilgi Yayınevi, 1968) (2 volumes). Also see Doğan Avcıoğlu, *Milli Kurtuluş Tarihi* (İstanbul: Tekin Yayınevi, 1974) (4 volumes).

42 Doğan Avcıoğlu, *Türkiye'nin Düzeni*, 69, 70.

43 Ibid., 70.

44 Ibid., 80.

45 Ibid., 79.

46 Samir Amin, *Delinking* (London: Zed Books, 1990).

47 Özgür Mutlu Ulus, *The Army and the Radical Left in Turkey* (London: I. B. Tauris, 2010).

48 Erik Jan Zürcher, *Turkey: A Modern History* (London: I. B. Tauris, 1998), 293–294.

49 For a recent study evaluating the US involvement in the 1980 coup before and after, see Ömer Aslan, *The United States and Military Coups in Turkey and Pakistan* (Basingstoke: Palgrave Macmillan, 2018), 166–187.

50 For the CTs revolving around the US masterminding an Islamic reaction in Turkey, see Doğan Gürpınar, *Komplolar Kitabı*, 154–170.

51 The classic text that "exposed" this scheme and popularized the CT was written by a retired military colonel who participated in the 1960 coup. See Haydar Tunçkanat, *İkili Anlaşmaların İçyüzü* (Ankara: Ekim Yayınevi, 1970), 43–57. The book was originally published in 1966.

52 Doğu Perinçek, *Eşcinsellik ve Yabancılaşma* (İstanbul: Kaynak Yayınları, 2000); Doğu Perinçek, *ÖDP'nin Kimliği: Neoliberal "Solculuğun" Eleştirisi ve Sosyalist Program-Siyaset* (İstanbul: Kaynak Yayınları, 1998).

53 For the making of neo-nationalism out of disillusionment from socialism, see Doğan Gürpınar, *Ulusalcılık: İdeolojik Önderlik ve Takipçileri* (İstanbul: Kitap Yayınevi, 2011), 265–271.

2 The Islamist counternarrative*

The Islamist historical narrative was centered on the presumption that the launch of Westernization itself was a conspiracy that was imposed forcefully by the West to loosen "our" morals and values and to disassociate "us" from our national past. This would make the Turkish people defenseless, feeble and misguided against Western transgression and was a course that was implemented by no lesser accomplices than those who ruled the country, beginning with Mahmud II (r. 1808–1839). The Tanzimat reforms were tantamount to an abandonment of the Islamic mores and culture that reigned over the moral landscape that secured the grandeur and splendor of the polity and the nation. The Tanzimat Westernization was followed by the Young Turk and Kemalist regimes on the same track, with the only diversion being the reign of Abdülhamid II (r. 1876–1909), who was seemingly deposed by the Young Turks but, in reality, by those behind them, that is, the Jews, Freemasons and Western imperialism. The Islamists long believed that the Turkish establishment (which they were certain existed as an intact and commanding entity since the onset of Turkish Westernization) had been under the influence of the Freemasons, Jews and Dönmes since then. The Bilderberg narrative that had become fashionable by the 1970s was also superimposed on this narrative, according to which the global superelite and the international Jewry were puppet-mastering their local accomplices.[1]

Under the partial influence of the Protocols of the Elders of Zion, the earliest Islamist texts sketched the contours of this scheme, and the framework would later be improved on, with claims that a cabal of conspirators including Jews, Freemasons and the imperialist West in capital letters were manipulating the Westernists and libertines. Necip Fazıl Kısakürek (1904–1983), a gifted poet who converted to Islam and Islamism from his youthful bohemianism, emerged as the most vocal Islamic public intellectual of the 1940s, having mastered and rebranded this narrative for consumption by the next generation.

The Treaty of Lausanne displayed a further example of servility to Westernism. Although the dichotomy drawn between Lausanne and Sèvres was quintessentially Kemalist, the Islamists were no less enthusiastic about exposing the causes of the imperial demise and national decay in a Manichean scheme. The Islamist version, however, blamed the Kemalists of subordination, arguing that Lausanne had been a betrayal and a succumbing to the British Mandate, amounting not only to a surrender in material terms (loss of territory, economic concessions) but, more important, an ideological capitulation and catastrophe as well.

The Abdülhamid cult

Abdülhamid II was the Islamist darling who allegedly upheld and invigorated the empire prior to being overthrown by the Young Turks (in 1909), who were seen as mere lackeys of the Jews and Freemasons in the Islamist account. The sultan symbolized the prowess, self-assuredness, manliness and resurgence of the empire, personalized in his stature, and this led to him being overthrown by an international conspiracy in which the Young Turks were deployed as foot soldiers, having been readily compromised and taken in by positivistic ideas, materialism, Enlightenment and secularism. It was no coincidence that the empire suffered an abysmal defeat at the hands of the small Balkan countries and an even greater rout in World War I, leading to the crumbling empire being partitioned just a few years after his ouster. Once Abdülhamid had been deposed, the empire was done, as had been foreseen by those very conspirators!

Abdülhamid II would be reappraised in 1918, the year of his death after nine years in custody. Although his overthrow was celebrated unanimously, crossing all ideological divides, after witnessing the horrendousness of Young Turks and their destruction of the empire in pursuit of vainglory, many began to harbor feelings of nostalgia toward the not-that-bright, but-still-stable Abdülhamid era. The prevalence of this mood during his funeral in February 1918 was conveyed in many accounts: "This was in fact the funeral of the empire". The following year, a pseudo-memoir of Abdülhamid II was published, ghostwritten by Süleyman Nazif, a diehard Unionist who had come to resent his political patrons who now fled the ruined empire in disgrace and humiliation.[2] The anti-Semitic publicist Cevat Rıfat Atilhan (1892–1967) also apocryphally quoted Enver Pasha, who allegedly resented Abdülhamid's toppling after realizing that his cohort had been wrought by the Jews: "We couldn't understand Sultan Abdülhamid; we were manipulated by the Zionists; we were exploited by international Freemasonry. So sad that we unknowingly operated in the service of Zionism".[3]

Yet the classical Abdülhamid hagiography that set the standard was Necip Fazıl Kısakürek's "The Great Khan Abdülhamid", published in 1965, which served to institutionalize Abdülhamid as a cult among the Islamists. Theodor Herzl's memoirs were partially translated into Turkish (only the parts pertaining to the Ottoman Empire) by Yaşar Kutlay two years later, who voiced his regret in the introduction that Turkish intellectuals still suffered from "inadequate knowledge of the relations between Zionism and Turkey", not grasping its centrality in the making of modern Turkey.[4] The bulk of this account would go on to be framed and reproduced almost verbatim by the leading lights of the Turkish conservative-Islamist intelligentsia. Primarily, it was the Jews that were seen as being behind the Young Turk coup. Their decision to settle in Palestine had been thoroughly condemned by the sultan, who even purportedly declined to receive Herzl in his court. He also allegedly expressed to his interlocutor Nevlinsky in no uncertain terms that "not a single inch of my lands is for sale . . . because this land does not belong to me, but to my nation". The meeting of Herzl with the sultan (five years after his first efforts to meet the sultan in person) in 1901 was a further blow to the Zionist schemer.

Realizing that they would have little opportunity to colonize Palestine as long as the formidable sultan remained in power, Herzl and his cabal considered the possibility of a coup. The link was so obvious that "whereas hitherto the constitutionalist movement was hazy, chaotic and obscure, it was transformed into a well-organized offensive subsequent to Herzl's dismissal by Abdülhamid".[5] Tainted with secularist, libertinist and positivistic ideas, the Young Turks became easy prey for the Jewish conspiracy, operating as willing accomplices. Alienated from their authentic culture, and hence losing their morals and consciousness, they would serve docilely as zombies and were easily manipulated by their puppet masters:

> As Abdülhamid II was well-aware . . . the Jews were well-disciplined and commanded power in different areas. They controlled international finance, trade and the European press. They first activated the European press and then galvanized the anti-Abdülhamid forces and instigated instability.

They also spurred a campaign of slander, and it was the Jews who dubbed Abdülhamid II the "Red Sultan" (*le sultan rogue*), a term coined allegedly in reference to his Armenian "policies" but, in fact, attributed perniciously by the Jews.[6]

For one conservative author, the mischievous intentions of the Zionists "had crashed the steel-clad stature of Abdülhamid II". For him, Abdülhamid II's overwhelming preoccupation in his office was Zionism, in that he not only tracked the Zionist network and activities abroad closely via the Ottoman embassies but also spied on the Zionist congresses.[7] Another conservative author maintained that "Abdülhamid conceded not even one single Zionist plea, even at the cost of his throne".[8]

The hostility between Herzl and Abdülhamid was so fundamental that for Ergun Göze, "poring over the memoirs of Herzl, one can gauge that this was an account of the duel [between Herzl and Abdülhamid]".[9] For Kısakürek, the Jew was the chief antagonist of Abdülhamid:

> One needs to look for the Jew in the background whenever one sees an organization or movement that slanders, accuses or attacks Abdülhamid, regardless of who feigns ostensibly on the stage. The chief antagonist of Abdülhamid was neither the Armenian, Muscovite [Russian], English nor the rootless Turkish semi-intellectual. His real and only and enemy was the Jew.[10]

For Necip Fazıl, this showdown involved not only a power struggle and maneuverings but also the moral, intellectual and ideological fronts. The Westernization fad was a mere Jewish scheme: "The pseudo-reformisms, economic and moral changes were all the Jew's bastards".[11] For him, all the agents of modernization were Jewish "institutions" including cosmopolitanism, Freemasonry, aping Westerners, servility to Western imperialism and moral degeneration: "The Jew succeeded in arranging the deposition of Abdülhamid II because he viewed him as the orchestrator of the moral and religious bulwark that protects us".[12]

The Abdühamid Cult for Samiha Ayverdi, another leading light in the conservative intelligentsia, "the era of Abdülhamid was the time when the battle between Jewishess and Turkishdom was at its zenith".[13] Abdülhamid was fully aware of the many "kinds of deceptions and machinations the Jews were undertaking to achieve Palestinian autonomy". such a shrewdness could hardly be observed with regard to the ill-advised Young Turks. Ayverdi was saddened that "those Turks who longed for a Constitution were manipulated, never questioning why neither Herzl nor Carasso [Emmanuel Karasu, the Jewish Unionist] were so ready to help them, regardless of the sacrifices and costs they paid". Likewise, in an anecdote related by Ergun Göze, after the coup in 1908 the Jewish subjects of the Ottoman Empire jovially and conceitedly affirmed that "[the Young Turks] could achieve [Jews'] ends for merely a few hundred thousand pounds, which [Jews themselves] could not achieve even for twenty million gold [worth]".[14]

The Armenians were also complicit in the anti-Abdülhamid conspiracy, and the reasons for their involvement were evident: "Abdülhamid stood against all of the efforts of the Armenians, succeeding in salvaging the

Figure 2.1 The journal hails "the three greatest antisemites of all times", noting that "the humanity is grateful to you". Abdülhamid II and Turkish anti-Semite Cevat Rıfat Atilhan beside Hitler.

Source: *Fedai*, February 1969

empire from the Armenian menaces and plots".[15] Hence, beguiled by their morbid rancor toward the sultan, the Young Turks unashamedly cooperated with the Armenians and became partners in crime. The extent of their treachery was such that they not only hailed the perpetrators of Dashnaktsutyun's failed assassination attempt on Abdülhamid as "the glorious hunter"[16] but also readily endorsed and used freely the slanderous term *Red Sultan* that had been forged by the Armenians.[17] Their treachery was made possible by their alienation from the moral, religious and cultural values of their society; their denunciation of their cultural heritage; and their moral debasement.

Young Turks, Jews, Dönmes and the Freemasons

The year 1908, when the Young Turks took power to their hands, marked the dawn of Islamic conspiracy theories (CTs). For them, it was vital that 1908 be undone and a return be made to the pure and unspoiled moral and political universe that existed before it had been despoiled and derailed. In that infamous year, the Unionists neutralized the sultan (deposing him one year later), which amounted to no less than a Masonic–Jewish plot in the eyes of the conservatives. Curiously, the ur-source of this CT was the British embassy building on the anti-Jewish and anti-Freemasonry CTs haunting Europe. A number of contemporary skeptic Europeans assumed that it was the Jews who were behind the Armenian genocide and that the slaughter was an extension of the economic warfare conducted by the Jews using the easily manipulated Young Turks. For John Buchan, the English novelist and the author of *The Green Mantle*, the Young Turks were "a collection of Jews and gipsies",[18] while Seton-Watson agreed with those for whom the main force behind the Young Turks were the Jews and the Dönmes.[19] It was no surprise that the Turkish conservatives would build on these CTs rendering the scheme native with a local flavor.

The nexus among the Young Turks, Jews and Freemasons was no conspiracy, as there were credible reasons for the establishment of such connections. First of all, the Young Turks used the Freemasonry lodges in Salonica for their gatherings, for both pragmatic and deliberate reasons, as the lodges, frequented by European nationals, were regarded as safe havens from imperial monitoring.[20] Furthermore, the Masonic ideals and culture were inspiring for the Young Turks, who shared the Enlightenment ethos of the Freemasons. The Young Turks hailed from Salonica (known as the Mecca of Freedom after the revolution), which was heavily inhabited by Jews and Dönmes. Jews constituted about 40% of the population of Salonica and were predisposed to the Young Turks against the rising Balkan nationalists who did not view the Jews in sympathetic terms. CT aficionados were to build a flawless scheme out of these nebulous facts and connections.

Gerald Fitzmaurice (1865–1939), the ambassadorial translator for the British Embassy trained for Oriental service, speculated on the origins of the coup as a devout Irish Catholic and concluded that the 1908 Young Turk coup was, in fact, a Jewish–German plot, aimed at threatening British interests in the empire. Not conceding economic rationality to the Young Turks, for Fitzmaurice it was German–Jewish economic interests that stood behind them.[21] "[Fitzmaurice] believed that in Constantinople things were not what they seemed, that political incidents had hidden implications and esoteric explanations".[22] The British ambassador Gerard Lowther was also no less scathing: "[He] . . . identified at the root of the Young Turk movement a cabal of 'Jews, Socialists and Freemasons', aided by the Jewish-controlled Vienna press".[23]

Emmanuel Carasso, a Jewish Freemason and a member of the Young Turk network, is referred to as an *éminence grise* in these reports, and as the coordinator of the nexus among the Young Turks, Jews and Freemasons:

> [This] low-class, and dishonest lawyer [Carasso], an obsequious, venal and secretive scoundrel, with a mysterious manner . . . appears to have induced the Young Turks, officers and civilians, to adopt Freemasonry with a view to exerting impalpable Jewish influence over the new dispensation in Turkey.[24]

Carasso was a Salonican lawyer of Italian Jewish origin and was a prominent Freemason, heading the Salonica Risorta Lodge. He had arranged the connection between the Young Turks and Freemasonry by providing the Young Turks with safety and secrecy through the Freemason lodges and gained further notoriety as a result of his involvement in the deposition of Abdülhamid II. To demonstrate the common will of the Ottoman nations, the decree of Parliament deposing the sultan was read to him in person by a committee of four, including one Armenian, two Muslims (one of being Albanian origin) and Carasso, representing the Ottoman Jewry. This overthrow of a caliph by a Jew was a source of humiliation and outrage for the Muslim pundits. Kısakürek bemoaned that "known for his hostility against the Jew, the sultan was imprisoned in a Jewish mansion in Salonica [Allatini Mansion], which was even more dismaying after the decree for his deposition was proclaimed to him by a Jew".[25] The presence of Carasso on this committee should therefore be "a caveat to those who cannot comprehend the real meaning of Freemasonry, and who naively reiterate the litany of friendship and brotherhood". For another conservative author, "this was the most embarrassing day in our history, and it should stand as an example . . . Awaiting all his life for this shameless moment, Carasso approached the sultan bursting with vengeance".[26]

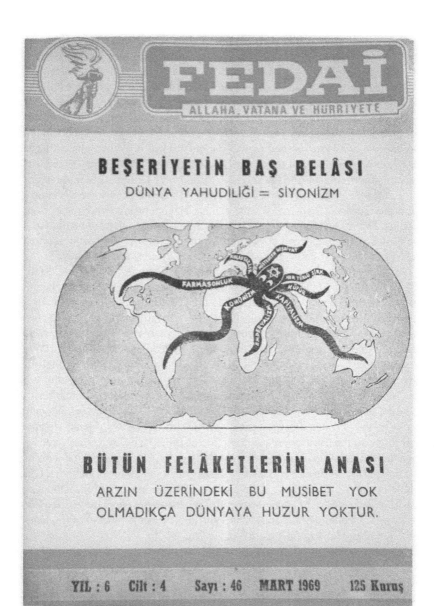

Figure 2.2 Labeling "global Jewry" as the "foremost nuisance of the world", the journal cover reminds its readers that "there would be no peace unless this menace will be eradicated".

Source: IDP (The Project for Islamic Journals)

The Sabbatians (also known as Dönme/converso) were descendants of those who had converted to Islam from Judaism following the conversion of Sabbatai Sevi, the Jewish mystic and self-styled messiah of the 17th century. The community had lived as a secluded community as a heretical sect in Salonika until their expulsion during the Balkan Wars.[27]

The fact that two Young Turk stalwarts were of Dönme origin was a bounty for the conspiracy seekers. Nazım (1870–1926; known as Nazım the Doctor) was well known (and feared) for his ruthless organizational skills as the shadowy iron hand of the Unionists, while Cavid Bey (1875–1926) was the minister of finance and the economic czar of the Unionists before resigning in protest at the entry into World War I. These liaisons were a bonanza for the conspiracy theorists, who saw them as conclusive evidence of their qualms. Derviş Vahdeti, Albay (Colonel) Sadık and Mevlanzade Rıfat were well-known and well-read conservative authors of the 1910s who accused the Young Turks of being a cabal of Jews, Freemasons and Dönmes.[28]

Yet it was Rıza Nur (1879–1942), the avid Dönme buster who established the frames of the Dönme narrative. After serving as minister of health and minister of education and after his break with the Kemalist regime in 1925, he devoted the rest of his life (but especially his highly conspiratorial four-volume memoirs, published more than two decades after his death) to debunking the Kemalist regime in general and Mustafa Kemal in person and exposing scandals (such as rife homosexuality and adulterous wives) among Ankara's ruling elite. In his memoirs, he incessantly mocked the "thick accent" of the republican stalwarts as an impeccable marker of identity, despite all their sinister efforts to conceal their ethnic origins, and spoke of the "broken *Dönme* accent of Mustafa Kemal". For Rıza Nur the real threat to the Turks were not the open enemies, who were easily recognizable, but those acting perniciously in disguise. These "enemies within" included all non-Turks for the racist Rıza Nur, such as the Albanians, Circassians and Kurds, although the foremost Trojan horse was the Dönmes, whose animosity to the Turks and their unabashed self-seeking maneuvers he saw as extremely obnoxious. The 1908 coup was the heyday of the Dönmes, yet Rıza Nur's main agenda was not the Young Turks of yesterday but the Kemalist elite in Ankara and, first and foremost, Mustafa Kemal: "He is from Salonica; he studied in the Military Academy; some say he is *Dönme*, for others he is Serbian, Bulgarian or Pomak. The hearsays about his father and mother are legion. One thing is evident; his maternity is assured but not his paternity",[29, 30] implying that his mother was a prostitute who gave birth to her son out of wedlock. Rıza Nur was not an Islamist but a blatant racist and outspoken atheist, yet his erratic memoirs were hailed by the Islamists as a secret history of the Turkish Republic in the genre of Byzantine Procopius's iconic *Secret History*, providing them with effervescent anecdotes and conspiratorial allegations.[31]

The prevailing Islamicate narrative on Young Turks, Kemalist and Dön-mes, however, was first constructed by Necip Fazıl Kısakürek in the late 1940s and would be perpetuated by the following generations of Islamist/ conservative intellectuals. The Young Turks' "shady connections and origins" theme was, in fact, a smoke screen allegory for an outright attack against Mustafa Kemal and the republic. Necip Fazıl spoke of "the false heroes" (*sahte kahramanlar*), referring to Mustafa Kemal and İsmet Pasha in Aesopian language, aiming to stir up the young people who attended his mesmerizing conferences. Kadir Mısıroğlu, Mehmet Şevket Eygi and Ertuğrul Düzdağ, among others, propounded further the Dönme theme.[32] The theme was carried on from the Islamic margins to the secular mainstream in the 1990s, which is another story that is recounted in the next chapter.

Treaty of Lausanne as a sellout

Lausanne was hailed by the Kemalists as the foundational document of the sovereign Turkish republic and, by the same token, sounded the death knell for the Ottoman Empire at the hands of the Western powers according to the Islamist counternarrative. For them, Lausanne had been devised by the British as a means of eradicating the moral tenor of the Ottoman Empire, in which the territorial losses of World War I were officially conceded by the Turkish delegation, while the New Turkey allowed itself to be demoted to the rank of an unassuming third-rate country. This meant abandoning its former glory, its imperial splendor and its pledge to address and lead millions of Muslims against imperialism and the West.

Haim Nahum (1872–1960) was the chief rabbi of the Ottoman Jewish community and was appointed as the candidate of the assimilationist Alliance amid broad protests by traditionalists and rabbinical corps.[33] Nahum thus symbolized the modernization and assimilation drive of the Jewish community being promoted by the modernizing Jewish party. He also befriended the British and the French, not surprisingly, due to the French appetite of the modernizing Jews, and was hence used by the Unionists as an intermediary even during the war, being seen as an asset by the Ankara government for his connections and for their efforts to demonstrate their reconciliation with the non-Muslims.[34] His brief attendance at the Lausanne negotiations with the Turkish delegation prompted conspiratorial visions, although the original source of these conspiracy theories was no less than the second delegate of the Turkish delegation, Rıza Nur, who in this memoirs recalled that

> [t]he ex-Istanbul rabbi began to frequent our hotel . . . One day I saw this seasoned Jew running into İsmet [İnönü] . . . From then on he never left İsmet alone. He knew when he would have lunch, appearing at the elevator door . . . Finally he approached İsmet with typical Jewish pushiness . . .

I told İsmet not to pamper to this Jew. That would impair the dignity of Turks . . . Don't you see he is in pursuit of his abominable interests.[35]

Although the gullible İnönü was unable to fathom the ominous intentions of Nahum, he was saved from being a toy in the hands of the rabbi by Rıza Nur. Yet although Rıza Nur argued that he had personally shunned Nahum from conspiring against the Turkish delegation, not everybody agreed. In 1949, Necip Fazıl Kısakürek (under the pseudonym Detective X) reopened the Nahum file, believing that Nahum had provided counsel to Lord Curzon during the negotiations. For Kısakürek, Nahum convivially relayed to Curzon that "the opportune moment to eradicate the religious tenor of the Turks had finally come".[36] The strategy was to divert the Turks from Islam and hence loosen their morality and stature.[37] Kısakürek expanded his allegations in the following year after İnönü's presidency expired, which made his harsh criticism and denouncement possible.[38]

One figure that is associated exclusively with the Lausanne theme is Kadir Mısıroğlu (1933–2019) – a prolific and eccentric Islamist public intellectual with a trademark fez (donned to thoroughly and visibly challenge and denounce Kemalist-imposed cultural codes and pronouncing himself as the "last Ottoman") that he was never seen without. Mısıroğlu published his most popular work in 1971, a masterpiece of alternative history in three volumes titled *Lausanne: A Victory or a Defeat?*[39] Although there he included a question mark in the title, Mısıroğlu entertains no qualms about Lausanne being a sellout. Identifying the losses of Lausanne as material and moral, it was the latter that was more tormenting. While the material losses included such territorial concessions as Western Thrace, Cyprus, Aleppo and Mosul, the moral losses were the privileges conceded to the non-Muslims and the continuing presence of the Greek patriarchy in İstanbul but, first and foremost, the abolition of the caliphate. This was essentially a renunciation of the claim of the Turks to the title of moral leaders of the Islamic world[40] and was much more severe than the material losses, being dictated by the British, who were happy to impair the moral compass of Islam. Although in the beginning İsmet and Mustafa Kemal stood against the abolition of the caliphate, they were forced to succumb after Mustafa Kemal met with Nahum in İzmir, who warned him that the British were relentless. It was not only Nahum who conspired during Lausanne, as Cavid Bey (1875–1926) was also a usual suspect, having served as an advisor in the delegation after being the finance minister of the Young Turks and had lived in exile for some time, and who was known for his pro-British views. Yet the most damning evidence of his treachery was his Dönme background.

Lausanne rose as an indispensable theme in the making of the genre of "the obscured history vs. the official history imposed by the republican elite" that prevailed among the Islamic intellectuals. Mustafa Armağan (1961–) emerged as the foremost public intellectual and dilettante Islamist historian, as not only a master, promoter and disseminator of "obscured history versus official history" genre and themes but also in terms of consuming and commodifying politically convenient Ottomanophilism. Armağan was not only a prolific (yet haphazard and distorting) essayist and author but also a major powerbroker with significant clout over the Islamist/conservative publishing houses and the editor in chief of the Islamist/conservative popular historical journal *Derin Tarih* (*Deep History*).[41] Armağan portrays himself as a myth buster, committed to the disclosure of the obscured history that has been distorted by the secular regime in a bid to drive a wedge among Turks, their past and their traditional moral values. Thanks to his strategy of debunking accepted history as a deliberate distortion, he freely amplified, promoted and spread conspiratorial historical visions, with one of his favorite themes being the Lausanne treachery based on Mısıroğlu's book and other sources of "alternative history". He was also one of the foremost champions of the Abdülhamid myth, further boosting it among the conservatives. His purported historical authority was also extremely expedient for the Islamist/ conservative historical challenge, assuring the Islamists of self-possession.

As a pupil of Kısakürek and Mısıroğlu, Tayyip Erdoğan's (sometimes opaque, sometimes blatant) constant references to Lausanne as a blunder kept the theme popular.[42] As the centennial of the treaty came closer, building on the enduring Islamic conspiracy theories on it, another anonymous one spread among the Islamic milieu according to which Lausanne had secret clauses that severely compromised national interests.[43] They were undisclosed due to the scheme maneuvered by the British to be able to dupe the Turkish audience, cajoling them that Lausanne was a good deal and a victory. The good news, however, was that Lausanne was effective only for a century as another secret clause stipulated. That means Turkey will be relieved from these (unrevealed) obligations once the treaty expires in less than a decade. Therefore, Turkey will be able to extract its rich (but unrevealed) natural reserves such as boron once freed from the secret clause that prohibited Turkey from doing so. Turkey will arise as a superpower, and it is no coincidence that the Islamist Justice and Development Party (AKP) is its Turkish abbreviation government will steer this course. The cessation of Lausanne will also denote the symbolic return of the Ottomans, caliphate and Islam as the driving force behind the Ottoman polity after one century of national ebbing.

Wahhabism as a British plot

The apocryphal memoirs of a British spy, a certain Mr. Hempher, were published by a certain M. Sıddık Gümüş, which was, in fact, the pseudonym used by Hüseyin Hilmi Işık, the leader of a Naqshibandi religious order known as the Işıkçılar (Işıkists), who adopted his surname. Building on the Turkish networks of religious proselytism, with teachings leaning on populist appeal and traditional Islam, Işık perceived Wahhabism as a threat that was alien and disruptive to local Islamic tradition and practice and published a number of anti-Wahhabi tracts to warn his audience since the 1960s reiterating the 19th century Ottoman anti-Wahhabi diatribes and even translated these tracts to various languages. He was further troubled by the Saudi incursion onto the Turkish Islamic scene thanks to the Saudi's seemingly charitable "Muslim World League (in Turkey known notoriously as *Rabıta* as short for *Rabitat al-Alam al-Islami*)" organization, founded specifically to disseminate Saudi Wahhabi Islam funded by overgenerous petrodollars.[44] Wahhabism was vehemently inimical to religious orders, seeing them as heretical and as diverting Muslims from the only true form of Islam that was strictly literal and Qur'an-based. This Saudi/Wahhabi threat had to be smashed at once, and the best strategy for this was to denounce it not only as a misinterpretation of Islam but also as un-Islamic and a ploy of the "enemies of Islam".

To this end, Işık revived the 19th-century Ottoman anti-Wahhabist animus, which was a response to the sudden rise of Wahhabism both as a religious creed and as a political force achieving territorial and military expansion. Following the notorious sack of Karbala, the Wahhabist surge was brought to an end by the Egyptian army, yet the radically innovative, puritan and ferocious Islam of the Wahhabis and their denunciation of all Muslims as apostates appalled the Ottomans. In response, Ottoman intellectuals responded to the challenge by disseminating anti-Wahhabi texts depicting Wahhabism as a corruption of Islam by treacherous, ignorant and fraudulent Arab tribesman. Penning treatises and refutations, 19th-century Ottoman historians and chroniclers (including illustrious Ahmed Cevdet Pasha Şanizade and later Şehbenderzade Filibeli Ahmed Hilmi and Hüseyin Kazım Kadri) fulminated against Wahhabism, seeing it as un-Islamic, deviant and heretical.[45]

Eyüp Sabri Pasha, a part-time author employed in the navy who had served in Hejaz and was knowledgeable of Hejazi affairs, published *The History of Wahhabism*, alongside a magisterial five-volume study of the Hejaz.[46] His account was recognized as the original source of the Mr. Hempher conspiracy in many references, although this is unfounded. For Eyüp Sabri, Wahhabism came into being as a result of the ignorance, seditiousness, moral corruption and fanaticism of the Bedouins, reflecting 19th-century Ottoman orientalism and the colonial aversion to the savagery of the desert Arabs rather than a British plot.[47] Yet applying a "respectable" Ottoman origin to this 20th-century forgery rendered it more persuasive and exalted.

The pseudo-memoir documented Hempher's assignment to Istanbul by the British "Ministry of Colonies" to master Islam, which he consummately did in his late teens, and was able to act incognito among Muslims. He swiftly learned three Middle Eastern languages to such a level that no one would understand his European origin when he spoke. After a few years, like an 18th-century James Bond, he was sent on a mission to Basra where he met Abdulwahab, the prospective founder of Wahhabism. Using his excellent knowledge of Islam to manipulate and distort it, he deluded the young Islamic cleric with his impressive Islamic knowledge and tempted him with gifts, women and alcohol, cajoling him that alcohol was not prohibited in Islam. This pseudo-memoir is also a classic account of an infatuation and captivation with British imperialism and its purported mastery of the requisite sciences and knowledge that have continued ever since (see the fantasies of the "British deep state" in the next chapters). The British were admired for their mastery of the intricacies of Islam to such an extent that they were able to manipulate it in line with their own ends and their imperialist ambitions, which the Muslims should have emulated to ensure the advancement of Islam.

This fiction was likely inspired by the "deeds and adventures" of the illustrious Arminius Vambery (1832–1913), the prolific and polyglot Hungarian Jewish Turcologist and orientalist. Vambery was based for many years in Istanbul where he not only mastered oriental languages, Islamic theology and the Orient but also traveled to Turkestan (Bukhara) disguised as a (fake) dervish, this being the only way of traveling to these "fanatical" regions without fear of beheading and robbery, like a 19th-century Indiana Jones. His flawless accent, mastery of Islamic sciences, feigning Islamic piety and even gestures could deceive the most devout Muslims, who were impressed by his Islamic erudition. Vambery was paid handsomely by the British Foreign Office for his regular reports on the intrigues, rumors and debates in the Ottoman capital and the palace, to which he had access as a result of his intimacy with the Ottoman elite.[48] His liaisons with the British Foreign Office gained him notoriety as the dervish spy among the Islamists and nationalists,[49] and this captivating imagery served to provoke such fantasies even further. Vambery was not the only Western scholar-adventurer who disguised himself as a dervish or a pious Muslim to travel the holy Islamic lands where infidels were forbidden to tread, extending from Central Asia to Hejaz, as Johann Ludwig Burckhardt (1784–1817), who became a student of the Qur'an and *fiqh* in Aleppo, with the aim of concealing his real identity and traveling the lands incognito and in fact died and buried as a Muslim in Cairo on his way to deep Africa with his tombstone bearing his assumed Muslim name. The British Richard Francis Burton (1853) and the Dutch Christian Snouch-Hurgronje (1884–1885) were other Western Orientalist-travelers who nominally became Muslim and even circumcised to be able to visit the Holy land incognito or not as Muslim pilgrims. Last but not the least, however, it was the Lawrence of Arabia imagery that had succinctly demonstrated the British capacity to rule by way of knowledge in the service of state and the inextricability of spying and knowledge.[50]

It was after the appearance of the forged memoirs that the denunciation of Wahhabism as a British design and plot to destroy Islam from within and partition Islamic realm really took hold and spread conspicuously to the Arab world. This dissemination was exceptional, as the diffusion of Islamicate ideas and discourse from Turkey to the Arab world was extraordinary.[51] Islamic discourse and fiction were most likely created in the Arab world and then imported by the Turkish Islamic networks. The Hempher story was reiterated by Muqtada al-Sadr's preachers, who argued that Saudi expansionism was no less than a British plot based on pseudo-memoirs at a time when Iraq and Iraqi Shiitism were under a grave Saudi threat.[52] The Hempher account was also recounted by Iran on the state propaganda news channel Press TV.[53]

This account also found a willing audience in Turkey, beyond the outreach of Islamism. This CT was even more conducive for the secular circles, for whom the Saudis epitomized the brazenness of political Islam but also the true face of Turkish political Islam. For many secularists, Saudi Islam was corrupted, contrasting the pure, morally upright Islam that was exclusively nonpolitical, seeking no earthly power and therefore compatible with secularism. The difference for the secularists was that Turkish political Islam was only cosmetically different to Saudi Islam, dismissing the rampant historical and theological antagonisms and rifts between Wahhabism and Turkish Islamic cultures.[54] Turkish political Islam also fit perfectly in the secular fantasy that imperialism and reaction went hand in hand, with the former playing puppet master to the latter. Serving their ideational constructs, this CT was widely disseminated among secular epistemic communities.

Conclusion

This chapter has provided an outline of the contours of Islamist CTs and their emotive reservoir. Rather than explaining the course of events and the shifts and transformations of ideas, it was more tempting to attribute them to an overwhelming conspiracy. These accounts denied agency to the Westernizing, liberal and reformist drive, as well as ethnic (Turkish) nationalism, presuming that they could not gravitate to such dispositions unless compromised and/or brainwashed. The Islamist narrative was first drawn up in the 1910s but was mastered in the 1950s, following the democratization and liberalization of free speech. Necip Fazıl Kısakürek was the chief disseminator of these CTs, giving them an authoritative imprint. Since then, these historical accounts remained almost completely the same with different authors reiterating the same themes and narratives with merely rephrasing. These themes also obdurately persisted and, in time, would affect Erdoğan's politics and Islamist rule. In fact, the young Erdoğan was a devotee Kısakürek like most of his generation of young Islamists. I expand more on these themes in the final chapter before delving into the rise of secular nationalist CTs in the age of global CTs.[55]

Notes

* This chapter is partially based on one of my chapters in my book in Turkish on CTs. Doğan Gürpınar, *Kompololar Kitabı* (İstanbul: Doğan Kitap, 2014). I thank the publishing house for the permission.

1 Yesevizade, *Bilderberg Group* (İstanbul: Kayıhan Yayınları, 1979); Mahmut Çetin, *Boğaz'daki Aşiret* (İstanbul: Edille, 1997).

2 Ali Birinci, "Sultan Abdülhamid'in Hatıra Defteri Meselesi", *Divan İlmi Araştırmalar Dergisi*, 2005/2, 179–180.

3 Cevat Rıfat Atilhan, *Türk Oğlu Düşmanını Tanı* (İstanbul: Ak-ün Basımevi, 1952), 46.

4 Yaşar Kutluay, *Siyonizm ve Türkiye* (Konya: Selçuk Yayınları, 1967).

5 Quoted in Mustafa Müftüoğlu, *Her Yönüyle Sultan İkinci Abdülhamid* (İstanbul: Çile Yayınları, 1985), 246.

6 Kadir Mısıroğlu, *Bir Mazlum Padişah: Sultan II. Abdülhamid* (İstanbul: Sebil Yayınları, 2007), 360.

7 Vahid Çabuk, *Osmanlı Siyasi Tarihinde Sultan II. Abdülhamid Han* (İstanbul: Emre Yayınları, 1990), 243.

8 Mustafa Müftüoğlu, *Her Yönüyle Sultan İkinci Abdülhamid*, 246.

9 Ergun Göze, *Siyonizmin Kurucusu Theodor Herzl'in Hatıraları ve Sultan Abdülhamid* (İstanbul: Boğaziçi Yayınları, 1995), 5.

10 Necip Fazıl Kısakürek, *Ulu Hakan* (İstanbul: Büyük Doğu Yayınları, 1998), 345.

11 Ibid.

12 Ibid., 346.

13 Samiha Ayverdi, *Türk-Rus Münasebetleri ve Muharebeleri* (İstanbul: Turan Neşriyat Yurdu, 1970), 233–234.

14 Ergun Göze, *Siyonizmin Kurucusu Theodor Herzl'in Hatıraları ve Sultan Abdülhamid*, 10.

15 Mustafa Müftüoğlu, *Her Yönüyle Sultan İkinci Abdülhamid*, 6.

16 For the Young Turks's praise of the Dashnaksutiun assasins, see Toygun Altıntaş, "The Ottoman War on 'Anarchism' and Revolutionary Violence", in Houssine Alloul, Edhem Eldem, Henk de Smaele (eds.), *To Kill a Sultan: A Transnational History of the Attempt on Abdülhamid II (1905)* (Basingstoke: Palgrave Macmillan, 2018), 121–123.

17 Altan Deliorman, *Türklere Karşı Ermeni Komitecileri* (İstanbul: Boğaziçi Yayınları, 1973), 72–73.

18 David Fromkin, *A Peace to End All Peace* (New York: Henry Holt and Company, 1989), 43.

19 Haluk Hepkon, *Jöntürkler ve Komplo Teorileri* (İstanbul: Kırmızı Kedi Yayınları, 2012), 158.

20 Thierry Zarcone, *Secret et sociétes secrétes en Islam: Turquie, Iran et Asie Centrale, XIX – XX siécles* (Milano: Arché, 2002), 81–106.
21 For Fitzmaurice, his political visions and impact, see G. R. Berridge, *Gerald Fitzmaurice (1865–1939), Chief Dragoman of the British Embassy in Turkey* (Boston: Martinus Nijhoff, 2007).
22 Elie Kedourie, "Young Turks, Freemasons and Jews", *Middle Eastern Studies*, 7(1), 1971, 90.
23 T. G. Otte, *The Foreign Office Mind: The Making of British Foreign Policy, 1865–1914* (New York: Cambridge University Press, 2011), 328.
24 Elie Kedourie, "Young Turks, Freemasons and Jews", 92–93.
25 Necip Fazıl Kısakürek, *Ulu Hakan*, 350.
26 İzzet Nuri Gün, Yalçın Çeliker, *Masonluk ve Masonlar: "İsimler, Belgeler"* (İstanbul: Yağmur Yayınları, 1968), 24–25.
27 For the history of the Sabbatian community, see Marc David Baer, *The Dönme: Jewish Converts, Muslim Revolutionaries and Secular Turks* (Stanford: Stanford University Press, 2010); Cengiz Şişman, *The Burden of Silence: Sabbatai Sevi and the Evolution of the Ottoman-Turkish Dönmes* (Oxford: Oxford University Press, 2017).
28 Doğan Gürpınar, *Komplolar Kitabı* (İstanbul: Doğan Kitap, 2014), 213–214.
29 Rıza Nur, *Hayat ve Hatıratım* (İstanbul: Altındağ Yayınları, 1967–1968), v. 4, 1515.
30 Ibid.
31 For the genre of secret history, see Rebecca Bullard, Rachel Carnell, *The Secret History in Literature, 1660–1820* (New York: Cambridge University Press, 2017).
32 M. Ertuğrul Düzdağ, *Yakın Tarihimizde Dönmelik ve Dönmeler* (İstanbul: Zvi-Geyik Yayınları, 2002); Mehmet Şevket Eygi, *Yahudi Türkler yahut Sabetaycılar* (İstanbul: Zvi-Geyik Yayınları, 2000).
33 Devin E. Naar, *Jewish Salonica* (Stanford: Stanford University Press, 2016), 102–103.
34 For a comprehensive biography of Haim Nahum, see Esther Benbassa, *Haim Nahum: A Sephardic Chief Rabbi in Politics, 1892–1923* (Tuscaloosa, Lonra: The University of Alabama Press, 1995), 1–45.
35 Rıza Nur, *Hayat ve Hatıratım*, 1081–1083.
36 Dedektif X Bir, "İfşa: Tarihin Çeyrek Asır Gizli Kalan En Büyük Hadisesini Buyurun", *Büyük Doğu*, 5(3), October 28, 1949, 3,
37 Dedektif X Bir, "İşte!", *Büyük Doğu*, 5(2), October 21, 1949, 3, 16; Dedektif X Bir, "İfşa: Tarihin Çeyrek Asır Gizli Kalan En Büyük Hadisesini Buyurun", *Büyük Doğu*, 5(3), October 28, 1949, 3, 16.
38 Dedektif X Bir, "İsmet Paşa ve (Lozan)ın İç Yüzü", *Büyük Doğu*, 6(29), 3, 1950 10–11.
39 Kadir Mısıroğlu, *Lozan: Zafer mi? Hezimet mi?* (İstanbul: Sebil Yayınevi, 1971–1975), (3 volumes).
40 For Lausanne and the abolition of the caliphate, see Mona Hassan, *Longing for the Caliphate* (Princeton: Princeton University Press, 2017); Nurettin Ardıç, *Islam and the Politics of Secularism: The Caliphate and Middle Eastern Modernization in the Early 20th Century* (London: Routledge, 2012).
41 For a study of the journal *Derin Tarih*, see Doğan Gürpınar, *Yerli ve Milli: Türk Düşününde Hamasi Söylemler* (İstanbul: Liberplus Yayınları, 2017), 192–209.

42 "Erdoğan: Lozan'I Zafer Diye Yutturdular", *Yeni Safak*, September 29, 2016; "Lozan Osmanlı'nın Defin Ruhsatıdır", *Yeni Şafak*, October 1, 2016; "Cumhurbaşkanı Erdoğan'dan Flaş Lozan Açıklaması", *Sabah*, January 28, 2018.
43 "Lozan Anlaşması Halka Açılıyor", *Yeni Şafak*, May 6, 2018.
44 Rabita's involvements and activities in Turkey following the 1980 coup were widely covered by Uğur Mumcu (for whom see the following discussion). Uğur Mumcu, *Rabıta* (İstanbul: Tekin Yayınevi, 1987).
45 Selda Güner, Vehhabi-Suudiler (1744-1819) (İstanbul: Tarih Vakfı Yurt Yayınları, 222-240.
46 For Eyüp Sabri Paşa, see Mehmet Akif Fidan, *Eyüp Sabri Paşa ve Tarihçiliği* (Ankara: Türk Tarih Kurumu Yayınları, 2011). Scanning his book on Hejaz, Fidan confirmed that no reference to Hempher existed in the book for which I am grateful.
47 Eyüp Sabri Paşa, *Tarih-i Vehhabiyan* (İstanbul: Bedir Yayınları, 1992).
48 Keith Hamilton, "Services Rendered: Arminius Vambéry and British Diplomacy", in John Fisher, Anthony Best (eds.), *On the Fringes of Diplomacy: Influences on British Foreign Policy, 1800–1945* (Burlington: Ashgate, 2011), 81–110.
49 Cemal Kutay, *Sahte Derviş* (İstanbul: Aksoy Yayıncılık, 1998); Mim Kemal Öke, *İngiliz Casus Prof. Arminius Vambery'nin Gizli Raporlarında II. Abdülhamid ve Dönemi* (İstanbul: Üçdal Neşriyat, 1983).
50 Thierry Zarcone, *Boukhara L'interdite, 1830–1888: L'occident moderne à la conquéte d'une legende* (Paris: Editions Auyrement, 1997); Geoffrey Nash (ed.), *Travellers to the Middle East from Burckhardt to Thesiger: An Anthology* (New York: Anthem Press, 2009); Cengiz Kallek, "Johann Ludwig Burckhardt", *İslam Ansiklopedisi* (Ankara: Diyanet İşleri Başkanlığı, 1992), v. VI, 420–421.
51 This plot was also briefly discussed in Daniel Pipes's book on Middle Eastern conspiracies. Daniel Pipes, *The Hidden Hand: Middle Eastern Fears of Conspiracy* (New York: St. Martin's Griffin, 1998), 211–212.
52 George Packer, "Caught in the Crossfire", *The New Yorker*, www.newyorker.com/magazine/2004/05/17/caught-in-the-crossfire?currentPage=all.
53 Simon Ross Valentine, *Force and Fanaticism: Wahhabism, History, Belief and Practice* (London: C. Hurst & Co., 2013), 281.
54 Arslan Bulut, "Suudi ile İttifak IŞİD ile İttifaktır", *Yeniçağ*, December 25, 2015; Hasan Demir, "İngiliz Casus Diyor Ki!", *Yeniçağ*, March 21, 2012.
55 For further elaborations on the Zionist–Jewish–Freemasonry CTs prevalent on the modern Turkish right, see Rıfat N. Bali, *Musa'nın Evlatları, Cumhuriyet'in Yurttaşları* (İstanbul: İletişim Yayınları, 2003), 279–385; Ekin Kadir Selçuk, *Mücadele Birliği (1964–1980)* (İstanbul: İletişim Yayınları, 2018), 137–180; Doğan Duman, Serkan Yorgancılar, *Türkçülükten İslamcılığa Milli Türk Talebe Birliği* (Ankara: Vadi Yayınları, 2008).

3 The neo-Kemalist conspiracy theories (2000–2010)*

The crisis of Kemalism and the birth of neo-nationalism (*ulusalcilik*)

After the then-reformist Islamist AKP (Justice and Development Party)[1] took control of the government in 2002, a radical response burgeoned among the seculars and secular public intellectuals that was fraught with avid anti-Westernist and antiliberal animus, as well as an anti-Islamist moral panic, in response to the dramatic shift of power. At this juncture, a new mold of Kemalism (that would become known as *ulusalcılık*, being a rendering of the word *nationalism* in Turkish yet sounding left and secular and which I hereafter use to denote "neo-nationalism") resurged and proliferated among the secular middle class and intellectuals.

This xenophobic nationalism was the self-styled only true form of Kemalism, claiming to trace a direct genealogy from Mustafa Kemal Atatürk and his political discourse right up to the 2000s. However, this appropriated form of Kemalism differed greatly from the mainstream Atatürkism that had prevailed from the 1950s onward in its sharp intolerance of ethnic and cultural diversity, its xenophobic nationalism and its blatant authoritarianism, which was in stark contrast to the conditional and pragmatic peace of Kemalism with democracy. That said, it was staunchly built on the Kemalist vocabulary and cultural affinities, and this predisposition was made possible thanks to the perpetuation of a mental mind-set that had been produced under the distinctive circumstances of a given historical juncture at a time of imperial retreat and the partitioning of the Ottoman Empire. Benefiting from a historical reservoir of more than a century, the neo-nationalist ideologues twisted the national narrative to suit their political agenda and rendered it the only legitimate and national program. Arguably, this shift was a symptom of the crisis of nation-statism in the age of globalization, as well as the rise of identity politics and pluralism. The hitherto consensual national narrative became conspiratorial in an effort to respond to and debunk the perceived threats.

The origins of this new indoctrination can be traced back to the "28 February Process" (of the late 1990s) when the Turkish military intervened indirectly in politics, first to topple the ruling coalition established by the center-right True Path Party and the Islamist Welfare Party and, subsequently, to redesign politics, the state and society while marginalizing political Islam. Rather than employing punitive measures and openly assuming political power, the military top brass opted to mobilize civil society by reshaping public "hearts and minds",[2] and this synergy nurtured a political climate in which neo-nationalist thinking proliferated.

The historical thrust of neo-nationalist conspiracy theories

The "whole world is against us" constituted the driving force of Turkish neo-nationalism (*ulusalcılık*).[3] This perceived enmity superseded the stigmatization of singular national foes like the Greeks, Arabs and Armenians. The Greeks and Armenians were no longer perceived as frantically seeking to fulfill their national aspirations, which were inherently antithetical to Turkish interests, but were considered rather as lackeys of an international plot to eradicate the Turkish nation-state.[4] The European Union and the United States began to be perceived as the foremost enemies of Turkey after the end of the Cold War, and it is worth recalling that Turkish–Greek relations began to improve and entered a friendly track beginning in the late 1990s, continuing ever since Greece lost its privileged status as the priority threat against Turkey. According to a 2010 survey, 37.5% of "educated" Turks regarded the United States as an enemy, with other "perceived enemies" being Armenia (10.9%), Israel (10.6%) and Greece (6.1%),[5] while another survey saw 46% of the respondents "tending to agree" with the statement "A crusader spirit shapes the character of European politics towards Turkey".[6]

Although the conspiratorial scheme formulated by the neo-nationalist intelligentsia was persuasive enough in the eyes of its true believers, it had to be historically proved and historicized, as "proving it historically" would make it scientifically impeccable, incontestable and irrefutable. The conspiracy theorists professed to being equipped with the requisite historical learning and self-assuredness feigning to deliver dispassionate rational inductions gleaned from history and iron laws of history. George Santayana's famous dictum "those who do not learn from history are doomed to repeat it" and Cicero's "*historia magistra vitae est*" maxim served as two bulletproof caveats dictating the unmistakable authority of history. Posing as modern-day Sun Tzus, they kept reminding that one should know history if one is to know about one's enemies and their strategies, which are much more subtle and pernicious than an average patriot can fathom unless trained.

Undertaking this mission, a steady flow of books were penned examining the late Ottoman period and early 20th-century Turkish history, uncovering the naked truth to serve as an example for the present, and many of these books became commercial successes. The conspiracy theories (CTs), the conspiratorial historiography and the themes contained within these writings were consumed with a passion by an attentive reading public, upholding the official Kemalist historiography but radicalizing it.[7] The sharp dichotomy drawn between the staunch defenders of the secular Turkish republic and its enemies within and abroad constituted their motivations, along with the underlying paradigm. These CTs also all presumed a level of coordination and tight cooperation between the co-conspiring enemies, both within and abroad, who were collaborating to destroy the secular Turkish republic.

The themes, premises and assumptions of these CTs are concomitantly novel and age-old and are derived from the lexicon and grammar of the founding nationalist ideology of the secular Turkish republic. All the circulating CTs were built on the preconceived historical setting and national episteme that perceived the course of the late Ottoman Empire and the Turkish War of Independence (1918–1922) not as part of a distinctive historical context but as recurring episodes in an enduring and eternal struggle between two unchanging and perpetually antagonistic parties. Playwright Turgut Özakman's (1930–2013) semi-fictionalized (novelized) narrative of the Turkish National Struggle, aptly named *Those Crazy Turks*, depicted the War of Independence in a highly chauvinistic language, and became a phenomenal best seller. The book became phenomenally popular among the middle class. Özakman inextricably interlinked his contemporary world to the historical era he fictionalized, reminding his readers never to overlook the overlap between the two seemingly different and distant eras.[8] The extent of this overlapping was such that these secular intellectuals could not desist from equating Western imperialism with the "crusader mentality" in quasi-religious ecstasy, thus rendering this clash eternal and permanent.[9]

The botched "reactionary" uprising of 1909 (known notoriously as the 31 March Incident among Kemalists);[10] the Sheikh Said rebellion in Kurdistan in 1925 protesting the abolition of the Caliphate which also carries Kurdish nationalist impulses, and hence seen as the paragon of the coalescence of Kurdish and Islamic concerns and subversions;[11] and all the Islamic unrest (such as the notorious "Menemen Incident" of 1930 near Izmir) were recounted as episodes in the ongoing eternal struggle that had to be approached with due concern.

Likewise, diverse and extraneous historical courses, moments and actors were all cast in this neo-nationalist imagery. The International Monetary

Fund was considered identical to the Ottoman Public Debt Administration (Düyun-u Umnumiye) that was established by a consortium of Western debtors to the Ottoman Empire to collect taxes in return of their debts and has since then gained notoriety in Turkish public opinion as the epitome of capitulation. The late 19th-century Public Debt Administration became the enforcer of the austerity measures imposed from abroad, as if in the age of neoliberalism. Nineteenth-century British imperialism was equated with contemporary US and EU imperialism. Furthermore, the contemporary liberals and left-liberals were equated with the late Ottoman Turkish "cosmopolitans" who sympathized and allied with the non-Muslims of the Ottoman Empire and, more perturbedly, with the appeasers of 1918 at the defeat of World War I. The Ottoman politicians, journalists and intellectuals who sought reconciliation with victorious Britain rather than outright renouncing British imperialism were associated with the contemporary pro-EU and pro-Western penchants and opinion leaders. Such late Ottoman intellectuals not only earned a bad reputation after the Ankara government's victory but were also indicted as traitors.[12] Khoyboun, a short-lived secessionist Kurdish organization founded in exile in the then-French protectorate of Syria in 1927 that was supported by the Armenians based in Syria who survived the genocide, became a showcase that was readily exploited by the neonationalists in the 2000s.[13] This organization served as undeniable proof of the historical prevalence of a devious collaboration between the Kurds and the Armenians (on the payroll of imperialism) against the Kemalist republic.[14] These historical references all served as gaudy references and lessons for the present day, history being a mirror for today that never misleads.

The antiliberal turn and the neo-nationalist epistemic universe

The foremost motivation behind the neo-nationalist surge was the lurking avid anti-liberalism. Although Kemalism had advanced an anti-liberal stance in the 1930s,[15] it was later tempered with the transition to a multiparty regime.[16] When the AKP assumed power in 2002, there was an immanent fear of its Islamic background. It is remarkable, however, how the contours of the anti-AKP discourse transformed over time. AKP began to be accused of collaboration with Western imperialism, while liberals and liberalism were incriminated for collaborating with, and even patronizingly manipulating and instrumentalizing, the AKP to their own nefarious ends. In the AKP, the neo-nationalists found the embodiment of the "double threats" of reaction and Western transgression. According to the neo-nationalist intellectual vanguard, the AKP and its Islamist baggage were espoused by the United States and the EU, given that their common enemy was the secular republic.[17] Moreover, for them the United States was actively engaged in the crafting of a "moderate Islam", seeking to dilute the secularism of the Kemalist republic.[18]

A novel anti-Western, antiliberal and xenophobic neo-Kemalist discourse was popularized through television shows, newspaper articles, Internet blogs and easy-reading political books. Infatuated with moral panic, the secular middle class and the hardline, secular, neo-nationalist ideological entrepreneurs were severely affected by this turn. Amid this moral and intellectual panic, the mainstream secular middle class drifted toward a heavily conspiratorial political vision, worldview and ideology as a result of their intellectual and moral Kemalist upbringing.[19] Ironically, this neo-nationalist ideology, originally advanced by ex-leftist intellectuals (as well as some right-wing nationalists), exploited the angsts of the secular middle class pertaining to the Islamic tide and hijacked it for their own xenophobic and anti-imperialist agenda through the intermediation of the Kemalist lexicon and political grammar.[20] Accordingly, the "arrivals" and "best-sellers" shelves in the bookstores in the well-off quarters of Istanbul, Ankara and Izmir began to overflow with books that were heavily laden with conspiratorial narratives.

In this decade, the AKP pursued pro-democratic liberal politics and a pro-EU agenda, in alliance with the minute but influential liberal intelligentsia, while the Kemalist opposition, represented politically by the main opposition RPP and intellectually by a self-styled Kemalist intelligentsia, were advocating a hardline nationalist and authoritarian line and advanced Euro-skeptic agenda.[21] The encroaching and deepening of the Kurdish problem, Kurdish militancy and the increasing political visibility of Kurdish politics and Kurdish nationalism spurred a nationalist backlash, blaming the Western powers, liberals and the Islamists for the "haughtiness" and self-assuredness of the "Kurds".

This epistemic universe fostered a conspiratorial vision of politics, the world and history for which the conspiracy theorists bestowed on their audience a "political kit", delivering self-serving and comprehensive answers to the quandaries of domestic and international politics and geopolitics and equipping their followers with the self-confidence to argue about politics. These CTs not only were manifestations of an ideology but also became the very building blocks of Turkish neo-nationalism, refashioning it as an encompassing, uncompromising hardline ideology with less tolerance of diversity. They became active agents in the molding of hardline secular nationalism and were fabricated and reproduced anonymously and collectively via cyberspace, websites, blogs, Facebook and forwarded emails (in the pre–social media age), resulting in the dissemination of conspiracy theories and alternative political and historical perspectives and thereby establishing their own reality and "regime of truth".[22]

A wealth of CTs exposing secret plots by the "global elite" (masters of the globe – *küresel efendiler*) to partition Turkey began to circulate on the Internet, as well as in the popular press and on TV, promoted by prominent pundits whose books had high readership. Many of these public intellectuals were ex-leftists or still-leftists, such as the aforementioned renowned poet Attila İlhan, popular journalist Soner Yalçın, professor of economics Erol Manisalı and idiosyncratic celebrity intellectual Yalçın Küçük. Many conspiratorial themes were exploited exhaustively, such as the activities of Christian missionaries in Turkey,[23] the alleged Greek claims in the eastern Black Sea (Pontus),[24] Israel's territorial claims (!) in southeastern Turkey,[25] the aspirations of the ecumenical Greek patriarchy in Istanbul[26] and the intrigue in the Vatican regarding Turkey. The "leading conspiratorial Vatican expert" in Turkey, who was also the leading "conspiratorial Greek Patriarchy expert", was Aytunç Altındal (1945–2013) – another former leftist who completed his graduate studies in Denmark on Christian theology and who devoted his time to exposing the incognito power and ambitions of the Vatican over Turkey and its efforts to manipulate Islam.[27] Not surprisingly, the EU was impugned of orchestrating these behind-the-scenes schemes that were naively overlooked or consciously obscured by the liberal intelligentsia.

A novel published in 2004 titled *The Metal Storm*,[28] fictionalizing a future US invasion of Turkey (and containing an emotion-laden scene in which Atatürk's palatial mausoleum was bombed) after a confrontation between US and Turkish military forces near Qirkuk over Turkey's rich mineral deposits, became an immediate best seller, leaning heavily on the anti-Americanism that was mounting over the US invasion of Iraq and its liaisons with the Kurds in Iraq (see Figure 3.1).[29] This was in a sense a Turkish Dan Brown moment, as the Turkish reading public was clamoring for easy-reading thrillers, esoterism and mystery to read while on vacation but with elements of neo-nationalism, anti-Americanism and militarism.

Although the themes of these CTs vary, the underlying motivations behind them were fixed, with all claiming that the governing then–moderate Islamist AKP was in the service of Western imperialists who were devoted to partitioning and obliterating Turkey.[30] Although the secular nationalists were staunch guardians of the republic, the Islamists entertained no loyalty in that regard and so would be indifferent to, if not elated by, the collapse of the republic at the hands of its enemies. Moreover, the marginal yet formidable and treacherous liberal intelligentsia championed this drift, stemming from their aversion to the nationally minded Kemalist establishment.[31]

This new captivation with CTs was also, in part, a corollary of the global appeal of CTs. Neo-nationalism and its conspiratorial vistas overlapped to a considerable extent with the conspiratorial visions surging elsewhere and,

Figure 3.1 Two of the neo-nationalist best sellers dominating the publishing market in the 2000s, one fiction and the other nonfiction: *Metal Storm* and *Entangled in the Web of the Civil Spider*. The *Civil Spider*'s cover depicts Turkish nongovernmental organizations and civil society as a spider net wielded by the West. The blurb on the cover by the neo-nationalist poet Attila İlhan introduces the book as a "slap in the face".

especially, in the United States.[32] The neo-nationalist epistemic universe in many regards resembled the US right-wing publishing industry's paranoid style in the age of Obama, not only in terms of content but also in the chosen medium. Although Turkish neo-nationalism is staunchly secular and anti-religious, as opposed to the religiously inspired new American right, they resemble each other not only in their exclusivist nativism but also in the means they exploit. Both created an exclusive epistemic universe, enjoyed a monopoly of a certain self-evident "regime of truth" and cultivated their own intellectual sphere that was closed to outside intrusions. They benefited from new means of media and communication, such as blogs, websites and newsgroups; they both enjoyed a booming publishing sector; and they were both self-referential.

The discourse employed by the neo-Kemalist intelligentsia and public intellectuals in print and in the TV studios, neo-nationalist TV hosts such as Hulki Cevizoğlu, Banu Avar and Erol Mütercimler and radio hosts such as Nihat Sırdar and Ümit Zileli resembled the bravado of Glenn Beck,

Rush Limbaugh and Ann Coulter in terms of their nostalgia, anti-liberalism and anti-elitism. They all detested the liberal intelligentsia, seeing them as indifferent to national values, sensibilities and sentiments and posing as mavericks against the elite, they presented themselves as guardians of national dignity. They were concerned not only with the coming to power of Obama and the AKP but also with the enhancement of cultural pluralism and diversity.

The transitions between the two are also remarkable. The main themes and premises of the American right-wing CT industry were imported and adapted extensively by the neo-nationalist intelligentsia. When Jonah Goldberg's *Liberal Fascism*, a book in the genre of American ultra-conservative anticommunism and anti-intellectualism and the epitome of the right-wing demonization of American liberals, was translated in the spring of 2010,[33] copies of the book were piled high in the "popular books" sections, among other such volumes. Goldberg's book was one of the first to popularize the analogy between Obama and Hitler, and it found a place alongside other tomes addressing middle-class sensibilities (such as books on Italian cuisine, pets, flowers and best destinations for summer holidays) and books on Atatürk in the bookstore chains that appeal exclusively to the middle classes, such as D & R, Remzi and İnkılap.

The Sabbataian craze

The "Sabbatian craze" of the 2000s mirrored well the twist of secular nationalism. As discussed earlier, anti-Sabbatianism had traditionally been the preserve of Islamists, while Dönmes had been assailed as false Muslims pursuing a hidden agenda. Islamists also tacitly (and falsely) implied that Mustafa Kemal Atatürk, who was born in Salonika, was of Dönme origin and, hence, that the Westernization of Turkey was a Sabbatian plot aimed at eliminating Islam from Turkish culture. By destroying Islam, as the cement in Turkishness, they sought to eradicate the Turks.[34] The Dönme theme was, however, brusquely rediscovered (in the secular public sphere) in the 1990s.

Dönmes and the Dönme identity of a number of public figures were an open secret that was deemed inappropriate for discussion in public debate, but this all changed with the turn of the 1990s. After decades of strict denials of identity, the 1990s witnessed the return of the suppressed. The Kurdish and Alevi identities came to the fore, much to the dismay of many, and the non-Muslims, whose historical existence in Anatolia and Istanbul had long been obliterated reemerged as a subject of public debate. In the decade of historical revisionism, the toll of ethnic cleansings and massacres perpetrated against the Ottoman non-Muslims prompted electrifying public debates, and this shift had also a nostalgic dimension, ushering in a longing for the bygone age of cosmopolitan Istanbul. In this atmosphere, ruminations and exposures of the curious and exotic Dönme community fascinated aficionados.

Ilgaz Zorlu, a young member of the community, not only outspokenly professed his identity but also protested the seclusion and denial culture of the Dönme community, calling on them to speak out. He also sought to return to his "real" religion and applied to the Istanbul Rabbinate to be admitted as a Jew (which the Rabbinate initially rejected).[35] Zorlu's Dönme "confessions" were a gold mine for the conspiracy busters, given the secretive nature of the community, their positing between two religions and the wealth, influence and prominence of its members that had enthralled conspiracy theorists.

Beginning in the early 2000s, two leftists, Yalçın Küçük and Soner Yalçın, played prominent roles in the popularization of the Sabbatianism craze in the secular milieu, advancing a conspiratorial interpretation of the history of the Turkish republic[36] that was centered on the systematic exploits and machinations of Dönmes and Jews.[37] Their favorite approach was to expose the baffling Jewish origins of celebrities, politicians and intellectuals through evidence procured from their very personal names (arguably, many

Figure 3.2 Two iconic conspiracy theorists with their trademark headgears as their political statements with which they appear in public: Küçük with a fur cap, the Kemalist headgear during the Independence War (1919–1922), and Mısıroğlu with a fez as an act of symbolic denunciation of Kemalism and owning Ottomanism.

names and surnames were Turkified versions of Hebrew names, epithets and allusions), their allegedly dubious connections and their family ties via marriage. Küçük thereby fashioned himself as a master of onomastics – the science of names.[38]

The conspiratorial (and anti-Semitic) books penned by Yalçın became instant best sellers, with his two books on the influence of Sabbatians in the course of modern Turkey, selling more than 250,000 copies (not including the tens of thousands pirated copies), and became iconic.[39] Furthermore, the blatantly anti-Semitic, anti-AKP trilogy of Ergün Poyraz, in which he purportedly exposed the Jewish origins of AKP stalwarts, became best sellers among the secular middle class.[40] These best-selling CT books depicted Turkish politics as an eternal struggle by the "good people" to defend the Turkish nation-state against the forces of evil who were allied against the republic. This alliance consisted of Islamists, liberals, leftists, Jews and the West (the European Union and the United States), and the leitmotifs of this conspiratorial fiction, more than being predominantly local artifacts, were exports from the international CT industry that all at once both partially and selectively resembled neo-Nazi, Soviet and American CTs.[41]

CTs of daily life

CTs related to daily life also entered the Turkish CT scene, with the twist in the Turkish appropriation of environmental and health-related CTs being their incorporation into the national conspiratorial narrative. For example, CTs on genetically modified organisms (GMOs) were firmly subsumed under the aegis of the nationalist framework, in which claims were made that GMOs, and especially seeds exported from Israel, were being used in a plot to fertilize and mutilate the genetic makeup of Turks.[42] As a leftist, he promoted, championed and amplified pronatalist conspiracy theories showing the interwoven nature of neo-nationalism. Climate change, soil erosion and looming natural disasters were associated with and attributed to intelligence wars and biological warfare, while dieticians, traditional medics and herbalists pondered on conspiracies in the food sector and modern medicine, turning their medicine-bashing into lucrative ventures.

The aforementioned Soner Yalçın, the iconic arch-CT disseminator of the 2000s, also shifted focus from overtly political CTs to those related to health, consumption and leisure, observing and gauging the new trends of the 2010s. His later best-selling book was aptly titled *The Hidden Elect*, in which he implied that "food industry barons" were the ones wielding power and governing the world from behind the scenes. Although the Rockefeller family, oil companies and the arms industry were all well-known holders of immense political power, the "food industry barons" were (in Yalçın's arcane language) the "hidden elect".[43]

He also "exposed" the global pharmaceutical sector, condemning their distortion and concealment of basic medical facts to sell more medicines and knowingly ravage public health.[44] He arrived at anti-vaccinationism by way of his health industry bashing, although as a self-styled leftist he held no conservative sympathies and predispositions. He also revealed imperialist plots within the food sector that were implemented by the medical and advertising sectors at the service of imperialism, in which the intention was to impair Third-World nations and countries like Turkey so as to subdue them to the throes of imperialism.

Traditional Turkish dietary habits were thus eradicated by the encroaching food sector, and the Turkish cuisine, based on olive oil and green vegetables (which is hardly factual, given that only a limited proportion of the Turkish population exists on a Mediterranean diet due to differences in climate and soil) was disparaged through systematic propaganda using popular culture:

> Through songs such as "I can't have Olive Oil", Turkish society was alienated from its traditional olive oil diet. This was one of the most popular folk songs in the late 1940s, and reached a wide audience thanks to the diffusion of LP records in Turkey under a wave of US cultural influence. Companies such as Columbia Records sold records such as "I can't Have Olive Oil" very cheaply in their thousands as a part of the instrumentalization of [popular] music as a weapon of US psychological warfare.[45]

Seeing it as unfashionable in the age of neoliberalism and market society, Turks were further compelled to abandon their traditional diet in favor of fast food, convenience food, unhealthy industrial foods, processed meat and junk food. Losing their organic and fresh vegetables and their seeds, GMO vegetables produced by the giant US food corporations took control of the Turkish market.

Sugar posed another imperialist threat[46] after the sugar factories opened by the Kemalist republic for the processing of sugar out of sugar beets were privatized or closed, and Turkey was forced to import not only sugar cane-based sugar but also, more heinously, glucose syrup. The sugar factories for the processing of sugar beet that had been opened by the young republic were presented as prime examples of the nationalist industrialization drive and an autarchic success in the Turkish elementary school curriculum. Accordingly, the privatization and closure of these sugar factories and the demise of the Turkish sugar industry as a result of its inability to compete with sugar cane and, more gruesomely, (GMO or non-GMO) high fructose corn syrup from the United States amounted to a loss of Turkish economic sovereignty. This loss was considered by some to be an act of treason against the Kemalist legacy in the hands of neoliberalism and the global food sector. The industrial food bashing hence lay at the intersection and coalescence of the nationalist narrative and GMO panic and fear, with Yalçın employing the latter in the service of the former.

Yalçın also blasted Starbucks and the many third-generation coffee shops that were cropping up in Istanbul and in other metropoles in the 2010s (with their hipster baristas). Starbucks, in particular, became increasingly associated with dandyism, hedonism and a disrespectful youth culture that had lost not only the Kemalist heritage but also any sense of social and national belonging. Yalçın argued in his book that whereas tea is healthy (Turks drink more tea per capita than any other nation, and tea drinking has come to epitomize the traditional Turkish way of life and taste, although it arrived in Turkey relatively lately and popularized only after the World War II), brewed coffee is very unhealthy, a fact hidden from the public: "Did you notice? There is an ongoing new perception management. You often hear 'tea is bad for your health and coffee is good'. They are now targeting Eastern Black Sea tea [Turkish homegrown tea]",[47] concluding that "global capitalism wants you to drink coffee!"[48] Apparently, the hostility to Starbucks and third-generation coffee shops was derived from their symbolizing of the hipster and urban youth subcultures, and frequenting these cafés was yet another symptom of the alienation from the Kemalist national consciousness. Starbucks-mania was not a fad but something that was consciously manufactured and promoted by the global food industry elite to change consumption habits and corrupt both minds and souls, rendering them frail against an imperialist onslaught.

Conclusion

This was a decade in which the AKP felt vulnerable against the national security establishment. The neo-nationalist public intellectuals began to counter the Islamic resurgence and mobilize their audience in the name of the nation, the republic and enlightened values, but they were to be thoroughly defeated. Things changed radically as the AKP took full control of the state and subsequently drifted to authoritarian politics. The secular nationalist conspiratorial intellectuals lost their public prominence, visibility and aura among the secular public, to be replaced by the liberal and progressive intellectuals who used the language of rights and liberties to disparage the AKP's authoritarian and increasingly anti-Westernist drift. The next decade, however, would witness the rise of Islamist CTs, accompanying an authoritarian drift that made neo-nationalist CTs look reasonable and naïve. As noted earlier, the semblances between the two milieus were many, yet they obviously represented two sharply different ideologies. After a brief interlude on ruminations and CTs on the deep state, I take a close look at the Islamist CTs in power.

Notes

* This chapter is partially built on parts of one of my previously published articles: "The Reinvention of Kemalism: Between Elitism, Anti-Elitism and Anti-Intellectualism", *Middle Eastern Studies*, 49(3), 2013, 454–476. I thank the journal editorial team for its permission.

1 For some assessments of the AKP, see Hakan Yavuz, *Secularism and Muslim Democracy in Turkey* (Cambridge, New York: Cambridge University Press, 2009); Hakan Yavuz (ed.), *The Emergence of a New Turkey: Democracy and the AK Party* (Salt Lake City: University of Utah Press, 2006); İhsan Dağı, "Transformation of Islamic Identity in Turkey", *Turkish Studies*, 6(1), 2005, 21–37; William Hale, "Christian Democracy and the AKP", *Turkish Studies*, 6(2), 2005, 293–310.

2 Ümit Cizre, "Ideology, Context and Interest: The Turkish Military", in Reşat Kasaba (ed.), *The Cambridge History of Turkey* (Cambridge: Cambridge University Press, 2006), v. IV, 310–314. For the emergence of a "Kemalist civil society", see Necmi Erdoğan, "'Kalpaksız Kuvvacılar': Kemalist Sivil Toplum Kuruluşları", in Stefanos Yerasimos, Günter Seufert, Karin Vorhoff (eds.), *Türkiye'de Sivil Toplum ve Milliyetçilik* (İstanbul: İletişim Yayınları, 2001).

3 For the rise of neo-nationalism in Turkey, see Doğan Gürpınar, *Ulusalcılık: İdeolojik Önderlik ve Takipçileri* (İstanbul: Kitap Yayınları, 2011); Onur Atalay, *Kızıl Elma Koalisyonu: Ulusalcılar, Milliyetçiler, Kemalistler* (İstanbul: Paradigma Yayıncılık, 2006).

4 For some examples of books that gained considerable popularity importing American right-wing conspiracy theories and adapting and localizing them to Turkey, see Erol Bilbilik, *Derin Dünya Devletinin Adamları* (İstanbul: Kırmızı Kedi Yayınları, 2009); Erol Bilbilik, *Dünyayı Yöneten Gizli Örgütler* (İstanbul: Profil Yayınları, 2009); Aydoğan Vatandaş, *Apokrifal* (İstanbul: Timaş Yayınları, 2009), Aydoğan Vatandaş, *Agharta* (İstanbul: Timaş Yayınları, 2008), İbrahim Karagül, *Hesaplaşma Yüzyılı* (İstanbul: Timaş Yayınları, 2007); Ali Çimen, Hakan Yılmaz, *İpler Kimin Elinde?* (İstanbul: Timaş Yayınları, 2000). Although some of these authors are conservatives, employing Islamic stereotypes and perceptions, from the 2000s onward the secular nationalists surpassed the conservatives in advancing a conspiratorial understanding of international politics, employing Kemalist stereotypes and perceptions to develop a conspiratorial worldview.

5 See "Eğitimli Kesime Göre, ABD Düşman, Azerbeycan Dost", *Radikal*, January 19, 2010.

6 Hakan Yılmaz, http://hakanyilmaz.info/yahoo_site_admin/assets/docs/Hakan Yilmaz-2007-TurkiyedeOrtaSinif-Ozet.28470911.pdf, 38.

7 For a study of republican high school history textbooks, see Etienne Copeaux, *Espaces et Temps de la Nation Turque: Analyse d'une Historiographie Nationaliste, 1931–1993* (Paris: CNRS Editions, 1997).

8 Turgut Özakman, *Şu Çılgın Türkler* (İstanbul: Bilgi Yayınevi, 2005).

9 For example, see Mustafa Yıldırım, *Sivil Örümceğin Ağında* (İstanbul: Toplumsal Dönüşüm Yayınları, 2004); Alev Coşkun, *Yeni Mandacılar* (İstanbul: Cumhuriyet Kitapları, 2008); İ. Reşat Özkan, *Yeni Mandacılık* (İstanbul: Ümit Yayıncılık, 2001); Erol Manisalı, *AB Süreci mi? Sevr Süreci mi?* (İstanbul: Derin, 2006).

10 For an example, see Doğan Avcıoğlu, *31 Mart'ta Yabancı Parmağı* (Ankara: Bilgi Yayınevi, 1969).

11 Although there is no substantial evidence that the Sheik Said rebellion was encouraged and supported by the British, it has been widely believed in Turkey that they were behind the rebellion and had initiated and encouraged it to allow them to keep Mosul and Kirkuk. For a semiofficial account of the rebellion and its suppression penned by the son-in-law of İsmet İnönü, see Metin Toker, *Şeyh Sait ve İsyanı* (Ankara: Akis Yayınları, 1968). For an academic study of the Sheikh Said rebellion, Ömer Kürkçüoğlu, *Mondros'tan Musul'a Türk-İngiliz İlişkileri* (Ankara: İmaj Yayınları, 2006); Robert W. Olson, *The Emergence of Kurdish Nationalism and the Sheikh Said Rebellion, 1880–1925* (Austin: University of Texas Press, 1989).

12 Attila İlhan (ed.), *Bir Millet Uyanıyor* (İstanbul: Bilgi Yayınevi, 2005), 9–32.

13 For depiction of such a nefarious alliance in the Kemalist era, see Ahmet Özcan, *Modern Türkiye'de Son Kürt Eşkiyalık Çağı (1950–1970)* (İstanbul: İletişim Yayınları, 2018), 77.

14 Yusuf Sarınay, "Hoybun Teşkilatı ve Türkiye'ye Karşı Faaliyetleri", *Atatürk Araştırma Merkezi Dergisi*, 14(40), 1998, 207–244; Yavuz Selim (ed.), *Taşnak-Hoybun* (İstanbul: İleri Yayınları, 2005); Abdulhaluk Çay, *Her Yönüyle Kürt Dosyası* (İstanbul: Boğaziçi Yayınları, 1993), 401–416.

15 For the speech of Recep Peker and the discussion following Recep Peker's speech to the Party Congress in 1937, see Murat Yılmaz, "CHP İlkelerinin 1937'de Anayasaya Girişi ve Liberalizmin Yasaklanışı", in Murat Yılmaz (ed.), *Modern Türkiye'de Siyasi Düşünce: Liberalizm* (İstanbul: İletişim Yayınları, 2005), 199–201.

16 See Cemil Koçak, *Belgelerle İktidar ve Serbest Cumhuriyet Fırkası* (İstanbul: İletişim Yayınları, 2006), 633–692; Cemil Koçak, *İkinci Parti* (İstanbul: İletişim Yayınları, 2010).

17 For books written by prominent public figures subscribing to secular neo-nationalism along these lines, see Erol Manisalı, *AKP, Ordu, Amerika Üçgeninde Türkiye* (İstanbul: Truva, 2008); Merdan Yanardağ, *Bir ABD Projesi Olarak AKP* (İstanbul: Siyah Beyaz Yayın, 2007).

18 Bahadır Selim Direk, *Küresel Tuzak: Ilımlı İslam* (İstanbul: Ulus Dağı Yayınları, 2008); Erol Manisalı, *İslamcı Siyaset ve Cumhuriyet* (İstanbul: Derin Yayınları, 2006); Yaşar Nuri Öztürk, *Allah ile Aldatmak* (İstanbul: Yeni Boyut, 2008); Cengiz Özakıncı, *Türkiye'nin Siyasi İntiharı: Yeni-Osmanlı Tuzağı* (İstanbul: Otopsi, 2007); Cengiz Özakıncı, *İrtica, 1945–1999* (İstanbul: Otopsi Yayınları, 1999). Although the term *moderate Islam* deserves a comprehensive study, it can be briefly stated to have derived from the Kemalist/Marxist premise that imperialism and the ruling classes always preferred and promoted religiosity and obscurantism.

19 For some studies on the rise of conspiracy theories among the educated secular middle class of Turkey, see Ali Bayramoğlu, *Çağdaşlık Hurafe Kaldırmaz: Demokratikleşme Sürecinde Dindar ve Laikler* (İstanbul: TESEV, 2006);

Ferhat Kentel, Meltem Ahıska, Fırat Genç, *Milletin Bölünmez Bütünlüğü: Demokratikleşme Sürecinde Parçalayan Milliyetçilik(ler)* (İstanbul: TESEV, 2007); Füsun Üstel, Birol Caymaz, *Seçkinler ve Sosyal Mesafe* (İstanbul: İstanbul Bilgi Üniversitesi, 2009).

20 For some anthropological studies on the political dispositions of the Turkish middle class, see Esra Özyürek, *Nostalgia for the Modern* (Durham: Duke University Press, 2006); Yael Navaro, *Faces of the State* (Princeton: Princeton University Press, 2002); Berna Yazıcı, "Discovering Our Past: Are We Breaking Taboos? Reconstructing Atatürkism and the Past in Contemporary Turkey", *New Perspectives on Turkey*, (25), 2001, 1–30.

21 For this process, see Nora Onar, "Kemalists, Islamists, and Liberals: Shifting Patterns of Confrontation and Consensus, 2002–2006", *Turkish Studies*, 8(2), 2007, 273–288. For an overview of RPP and its crisis, see Sinan Ciddi, *Kemalism in Turkish Politics: The Republican People's Party, Secularism and Nationalism* (London, New York: Routledge, 2009); Yunus Emre, *The Emergence of Social Democracy in Turkey* (London: I. B. Tauris, 2014).

22 For the online anti-Semitism in Turkey, see Türkay Salim Nefes, *Online Anti-Semitism in Turkey* (Basingstoke: Palgrave Macmillan, 2015).

23 "'AB'ye Gireceğiz Diye Dinimiz Elden Gidiyor'", *Sabah*, January 3, 2005.

24 Yusuf Sarınay, Hamit Pehlivanlı, Abdullah Saydam, *Pontus Meselesi ve Yunanistan'ın Politikası* (Ankara: Atatürk Araştırma Merkezi, 1999); Arslan Bulut, *Çift Başlı Yılan: Karadeniz'de Yüzyılın İkinci Rumlaştırma Operasyonu* (İstanbul: BilgeOğuz, 2007). For a study of the Pontus paranoia, see Ömer Asan, "Trabzon Rumcası ve Pontos Etnofobisi", in Güven Bakırezer, Yücel Demirer (eds.), *Trabzon'u Anlamak* (İstanbul: İletişim Yayınları, 2009).

25 "GAP'ta İkinci Filistin Oyunu", *Sabah*, June 13, 2006.

26 Aytunç Altındal, *Türkiye ve Ortodokslar* (İstanbul: Anahtar Kitaplar, 2005); Sadi Somuncuoğlu, *İstanbul'da Yeni Roma İmparatorluğu* (Ankara: Akçağ Yayınları, 2004); Uğur Yıldırım, *Dünden Bugüne Patrikhane* (İstanbul: Kaynak Yayınları, 2004).

27 See, Aytunç Altındal, *Papa XVI. Benedikt. Gizli Türkiye Gündemi* (İstanbul: Destek Yayınları, 2006); Aytunç Altındal, *Vatikan ve Tapınak Şövalyeleri* (İstanbul: Alfa Yayınları, 2005); Aytunç Altındal, *Üç İsa* (İstanbul: Anahtar Kitaplar, 1993).

28 Burak Turna, Orkun Uçar, *Metal Fırtına* (İstanbul: Timaş Yayınları, 2004).

29 For another conspiratorial nonfiction study benefiting from the tensions mounting over the US presence and engagement in Kurdish Northern Iraq, see Ahmet Erimhan, *Çuvaldaki Müttefik* (İstanbul: Birharf, 2006).

30 For the secular Euroskepticism of the time, see Hakan Yılmaz, *Türkiye'de Orta Sınıfı Tanımlamak* (Boğaziçi: Üniversitesi Bilimsel Araştırma Projeleri ve Açık Toplum Enstitüsü Projesi, 2007), 8, http://hakanyilmaz.info/yahoo_site_admin/assets/docs/HakanYilmaz-2007-TurkiyedeOrtaSinif-Ozet.28470911.pdf (retrieved September 11, 2010). Yılmaz prefers to define the top 22% of Turkish society as the upper class (*üst sınıf*) rather than (upper) middle class.

31 For some popular and widely read neo-nationalist books assailing the liberal intelligentsia and accusing them of treason, see Mustafa Yıldırım, *Sivil Örümceğin Ağında* (İstanbul: Toplumsal Dönüşüm Yayınları, 2004); Necip Hablemitoğlu, *Alman Vakıfları: Bergama Dosyası* (İstanbul: Otopsi Yayınları, 2001); Necip Hablemitoğlu, *Şeriatçı Terörün ve Batının Kıskacındaki Ülke: Türkiye* (İstanbul: Toplumsal Dönüşüm Yayınları, 2003).

32 For a thorough study of the Tea Party movement as a response to the presidency of Barack Obama, see Theda Skocpol, Vanessa Williams, *The Tea Party and the Remaking of Republican Conservatism* (Oxford, New York: Oxford University Press, 2012). For the patriotic historical visions of the Tea Party activists which resemble the conspiratorial interpretation of "patriotic history" and the emotional bond Turkish secular neo-nationalists forged with the Kemalist regime, see Jill Lepore, *The Whites of Their Eyes: The Tea Party's Revolution and the Battle Over American History* (Princeton: Princeton University Press, 2010).

33 For the translation of Jonah Goldberg's *Liberal Fascism*, see Jonah Goldberg, *Liberal Faşizm* (İstanbul: Pegasus, 2010).

34 Rıfat Bali, *A Scapegoat for All Seasons: The Dönmes or Crypto-Jews of Turkey* (İstanbul: Isis, 2008), 17–78.

35 Ilgaz Zorlu, *Evet, Ben Selanikliyim* (İstanbul: Belge Yayınları, 1998).

36 Soner Yalçın, *Efendi: Beyaz Türklerin Büyük Sırrı* (İstanbul: Doğan Kitapçılık, 2004); Soner Yalçın, *Efendi 2: Beyaz Müslümanların Büyük Sırrı* (İstanbul: Doğan Kitapçılık, 2007); Yalçın Küçük, *Putları Yıkıyorum* (İstanbul: İthaki, 2004); Yalçın Küçük, *Tekelistan* (İstanbul: YGS Yayınları, 2002); Yalçın Küçük, *Şebeke* (İstanbul: YGS Yayınları, 2002); Yalçın Küçük, *İsyan* (İstanbul: İthaki, 2005).

37 For the anti-Semitism of Soner Yalçın's books, also see Necati Polat, "Yeni Anti-Semitizm: Efendi Üzerine Notlar", *Doğu-Batı*, 7(29), 2004, 179–194; Rıfat Bali, "What Is *Efendi* Telling Us?" in Rıfat Bali (ed.), *A Scapegoat for All Seasons: The Dönmes or Crypto-Jews of Turkey* (İstanbul: Isis, 2008), 317–349.

38 Yalçın Küçük, *Fitne* (İstanbul: Mızrak, 2010).

39 Rıfat Bali, *A Scapegoat for All Seasons: The Dönmes or Crypto-Jews of Turkey* (İstanbul: Isis, 2008), 12–13.

40 Ergun Poyraz, *Musa'nın Çocukları* (İstanbul: Togan Yayıncılık, 2007); Ergun Poyraz, *Musa'nın Gülü* (İstanbul: Togan Yayıncılık, 2007); Ergun Poyraz, *Musa'nın Mücahidi* (İstanbul: Togan Yayıncılık, 2007). Turgut Özakman, *Şu Çılgın Türkler* (İstanbul: Bilgi Yayınevi, 2005).

41 For the American right-wing conspiracy theory industry, see Robert Alan Goldberg, *Enemies Within* (New Haven: Yale University, 2001); Michael Barkun, *A Culture of Conspiracy* (Berkeley: University of California Press, 2003); Peter Knight, *Conspiracy Culture: American Paranoia From Kennedy to the 'X-Files'* (New York: Routledge, 2001); Mark Fenster, *Conspiracy Theories: Secrecy and Power in American Culture* (Minneapolis, London: University of Minnesota Press, 2008); Kathryn S. Olmsted, *Real Enemies: Conspiracy Theories and American Democracy, World War I to 9/11* (Oxford: Oxford University Press, 2009).

42 Doğan Gürpınar, *Komplolar Kitabı* (İstanbul: Doğan Kitap, 2014), 192–193.

43 Soner Yalçın, *Saklı Seçilmişler* (İstanbul: Kırmızı Kedi, 2017).

44 Industrial food panic is obviously a modern fear. See Harvey Levenstein, *Fear of Food* (Chicago: The University of Chicago Press, 2012).

45 Soner Yalçın, *Saklı Seçilmişler*, 279–280. The laying of the blame for the aforementioned folk tune at the door of US food imperialism belonged to Osman Nuri Koçman (1918–1994). Originally a veterinary surgeon serving in the army as a veterinary officer, he would later teach at a university and work for the government as an expert. While the leftist youth was organizing protests in defense of the olive farmers in the Aegean in the late 1960s, he penned a pamphlet, as requested by the organizing committee, in which he "revealed"

the imperialistic motivation behind the folk song. See Osman Arolat, *Bir Gençlik Liderinin Anıları, 1959–1974* (İstanbul: İş Bankası Yayınları, 2018), 40–41. Koçman published numerous books that blasted Marshall aid (due to the foods sent as part of the aid), US agro-industry and the shaping of Turkish agricultural policies according to imperialist interests. The anti-imperialist Koçman's writings inspired not only the anti-imperialistic youth, debunking the US food sector engaged in Turkey, but also Soner Yalçın, for whom Koçman was a major source for his book. See also Soner Yalçın, "CIA'in Hedefindeki Gıda Uzmanı: Tarhana Osman", *Sözcü*, November 16, 2014. I thank Erkan Şen for notifying me of this connection. For another book along the same lines, see S. Serpil Özkaynak, *Türk Tarımının Bilinçli Yok Edilişi* (İstanbul: Yayın B, 2010). The book's subtitle is revealingly: "The Agricultural Dimensions of the Civil Spider," named after a conspiratorial best-selling title *Entangled in the Web of the Civil Spider* by Mustafa Yıldırım, benefiting from the metaphorical cover of the earliest prints of Elders of Zion in which Jews are nesting web through the globe as if a spider.
46 Soner Yalçın, *Saklı Seçilmişler*, 89–90.
47 Ibid., 241.
48 Ibid., 243.

4 Deep state

Reality, discourse, conspiracy theory

The "deep state", both as a reality and as a discourse, was an original contribution by Turkey to the global conspiracy theory (CT) community and political intrigue *aficionados*. The term, in fact, metamorphosed from the hideous term *counterguerrilla* (*Kontrgerilla*) that disseminated among the leftist activists arrested during the martial law (1971–1973) as the nefarious authority that runs the brutal crackdown and interrogations.[1] Central Intelligence Agency (CIA) was also accused as behind the counterguerrilla that professionally runs tortures as an effective counterinsurgency technique.[2] İlhan Selçuk (aforementioned in Chapter 1) is renowned for hearing the notorious word *counterguerrilla* in person when he was brought to a mansion in Istanbul owned by the Turkish intelligence and used for interrogation. As he recalled in his memoirs, blindfolded, he was welcomed by his interrogators (and to-be-torturers):

> Mr. İlhan Selçuk, now you are in front of the Counter-guerilla organization run by the General Staff. You are our captive. There is no Constitution here. We are authorized to do anything to you. . . . I am a colonel. My colleague is also a colonel. We will interrogate you. Don't dare to resist. We have handled thousands just like you.[3]

Bülent Ecevit, the incoming leftist prime minister after the end of the military-run martial law, further dispersed the term referring to it in a political rally in 1974. He articulated the term after becoming aware of a private branch within the government that was unaccountable to political authority after being asked to approve of the channeling of discretionary funds under his aegis but advised not to inquire into their purpose by the military generals.[4] Ecevit fulminated against the state-within-state order, identifying it as counterguerrilla and positing himself and his leftist stand in direct conflict with this security establishment. Since then, leftists in Turkey have used the term often to refer to structures outside the reach of political accountability and visibility whose main role was to counter and repress leftist subversion through extralegal and unaccountable means.

This was, in fact, the Turkish branch of a North Atlantic Treaty Organization (NATO)–wide stay-behind organization, the clandestine connections of which were first revealed in Italy,[5] although the Turkish case seems to have differed slightly.[6] The body was well incorporated into the inherited authoritarian bureaucratic system and became, inevitably, its constitutive part, persisting after the Cold War but with the new mission of "defending" the state not from the communist menace but from other perceived subversive threats. Whereas the stay-behind schemes were silently eliminated in other NATO countries, the Turkish wing survived but was directed toward other perceived threats.

As the Kurdistan Worker's Party (PKK) – a Kurdish separatist terrorist organization – surged as a major threat, extralegal measures began to be employed. Back in the 1970s, young people were recruited from the right wing as paramilitary operatives (including Mehmet Ali Ağca, who would go on to gain international fame for the assassination attempt against the pope), but as these young people came of age, they evolved from being hitmen who took orders into agents of power. Many of the paramilitaries turned their hand to organized crime using their acquired violence and intimidation skills after losing their purpose following the military coup in 1980 that all but stamped out leftist militancy. The PKK's control of heroin trafficking across the eastern borders triggered a state response of cooperating with ex-right-wing paramilitaries that were by that time running mafia networks. Notorious mobsters such as Alaattin Çakıcı, Tevfik Ağansoy, Ali Yasak (Drej Ali), former far-right militants, now controlled vast networks of violence operating with the tacit approval of the state.[7]

The term *counterguerrilla* gave way abruptly to the phrase "deep state" in late 1996 after a curious car accident in the countryside that exposed a matrix of power at the intersection of the state security establishment, mafia networks and other shady connections. The strange bedfellows who died in the crash included one police chief, one wanted criminal (Abdullah Çatlı [1956–1996], who had vanished without a trace ten years earlier) and one beauty queen. The fourth passenger, who survived, was a parliamentary deputy who owed his political office to his commanding a Kurdish tribe and his loyalty to the state in its counterinsurgency warfare against the PKK. Çatlı's name on the list appalled many, especially the leftists who recalled his name from the tumultuous 1970s when he headed the youth section of the far-right Nationalist Movement Party and a paramilitary chief and fled abroad after being accused of being behind two massacres of leftist activists. Ostensibly working for Turkish Foreign Intelligence, he was later imprisoned in France, summoned as a witness in the trial of Ağca for the attempted assassination of John Paul II, escaped a Swiss prison in 1990, and was on the missing list until his corpse was identified in the crash traveling under a fake ID. The phrase "deep state" entered into circulation following the notorious accident amid these appalling exposures. The phrase was first used in 1995 by Ertuğrul Özkök, the flamboyant editor in chief of mainstream Turkish newspaper *Hürriyet*, who later attributed the term to Mehmet Ağar – a police chief and *éminence grise* of the deep state who had murmured about the "reflexes of deep state" to Özkök at a dinner.[8] Özkök claimed to adore the term, as it reminded him of the French phrase *La France profonde* inferring the provincial France vis-à-vis metropolitan and cosmopolitan Paris in his condescending habit of demonstrating his Francophony. The phrase immediately became a household term, thanks to its immense power and capacity to infer the dreadful and captivating imagery of the network of connections condensed in one heavily loaded buzzword.

Uğur Mumcu (1942–1993), a leftist journalist who was killed in 1993 in a mysterious car bomb whose perpetrators and motivations still remain unknown (thus himself presumedly another victim of the 'deep state'), wrote consistently and succinctly about and sought-after Çatlı and his connections in the 1980s.[9] Mumcu's books and researches were impressive and daring, making him an icon and paragon of investigative journalism. Yet others cast doubt on his conduct, pointing out to his unidentified sources, who were supposedly from the top echelons of the national security establishment. He was also impugned for harboring close ties with the top military brass and the commanders of the 1980 junta, despite his staunch leftist convictions. It looked like Mumcu was using his close ties with the military's leftist factions, who acted as "deep throats" in the provision of valuable inside information.

Inspired by Mumcu's mastery of the art, in the 1990s, "deep state revelations" became an intriguing genre fashionable among mostly leftist journalists – some mediocre and posing and others seasoned, courageous and breathtaking. Yet these revelations were, in fact, reverberations from the ongoing battles between factions in the "deep state" (mainly left-wing and right-wing factions but also organized over networks and personalized connections and allegiances). This was best crystallized in the leak and publication of a top-secret Turkish intelligence report in the leftist weekly *2000'e Doğru* (*Towards 2000*) in 1988, highlighting the outrageous mafia and state intelligence connections as an offshoot of interfactional feuds. The "deep state" hence served also as a discourse, functioning as a ploy amid the power struggles in which many "deep state exposers" were inadvertently manipulated and instrumentalized.

Although it was serious journalism for some, by the 2000s it had for many become pure fantasy fiction. Aspirant intellectuals gained instant celebrity, respect and intellectual stature as self-styled "deep state experts", with the common trick being to infer that you know much more than you can openly reveal, with an aura of mystery. Quoting from the fictional characters he surveyed in his study of "US covert space", meaning the constellation of state bodies operating shrouded in secrecy including the National Security Agency (NSA), the CIA and the Federal Bureau of Investigation (FBI), Thomas Melley assessed how this secrecy fascinated the onlookers: "The covert state has become a primary force in the postmodern 'reenchantment of the World . . . it is 'America's myth', a 'theology of secrets' whose 'holy men are . . . a secret fraternity of the American political aristocracy".[10] He named this fiction genre as "geopolitical melodrama".[11] The Turkish fantasizing about "deep state" also sparked a host of "geopolitical melodrama".

The TV series *Kurtlar Vadisi* (*Valley of the Wolves*) that began to be screened in 2001 and became probably the most popular series ever in Turkey was a fictionalization and aestheticization of the "deep state" that was heavily influenced by the Tarantino-esque aesthetics of violence.[12] The conspiratorial cabal met regularly (The Council of the Wolves) to run their empire of influence (see Figure 4.1). Once a promising asset of Turkish intelligence, the cabal and the Council of Wolves was headed by Mehmet Karahanlı, also known as The Baron, who was recruited by a Templar-like global organization and switched sides. This conspiracy was countered by those elements of the "deep state" imbued with the time-honored

Figure 4.1 The series *Valley of the Wolves* as deep state chronicles. The Council of the Wolves in meeting conspiring and chaired by Mehmet Karahanlı in the center, known as Baron.

state culture. One side (but key) character, known as Aslan Bey after his alias, personified this wisdom arguably fictionalized from a real-life (assassinated) Turkish intelligence chief. The allure of the series, in fact, derived from the discreet allusions to real-life characters that beguiled the viewers seeing the series as a guide to grasp the political and geopolitical intricacies by just watching TV. In fact, the shooting of the episodes were finished one day before the TV screening to be able to incorporate any last minute development to the episode to feign as the series is foreseeing the course of events. The series is full of "wisdom talk" that invoked sagacity and acumen, filtering through the Turkish state-building culture of hundreds of years. The series' political sympathies (and allegiances) also shifted in time as Gülenist and Justice and Development Party (AKP) imprint came to be felt and radically transformed the contours of the series from its original neo-nationalist pillars as a corollary of shifts of political power. Following this shift, esoteric elements became more manifest in the series (see Figure 4.2).

While for some the "deep state" is an evil dark force scheming behind closed doors, for others it is not only tempting as a Turkish and real-life James Bond world, bursting with patriotic zeal, but also the incarnation of the 2,000 years of "Turkish state culture", boosting pride in the nation's proud sons. The deep state operatives in the series displayed role models for those wannabe ruffians feigning as swashbucklers seeking to associate

Figure 4.2 The Illuminati in session in the *Valley of the Wolves.*

themselves with the state and amalgamating their machismo with self-styled patriotism. One fictive institution introduced to the series was the Council of Elders headed by a White-Haired (*Aksaçlı*). This council protects the state interests from time immemorial as a Turkic institution. As this fiction fit the popular historical fantasies, it was widely taken as a real-life organization and thus tantamount to institutionalized deep state prevailing throughout centuries. This mythical council was later incorporated by the TV series Resurgence (*Diriliş*), a historical drama set in the still nomadic Ottoman principality created as a AKP nationalist propaganda outlet. The council this time appears as White-Beards guarding the Turkic cause and allegedly played a prominent role in transmitting the Turkic (or Turco-Islamic befitting AKP's agenda) mandate to the house of Osman. It is also noteworthy that this series was seen by its audience as a documentary instructing historical reality.

Whereas the "deep state revelation" genre was predominantly a leftist pursuit, by the 2000s Islamists had also taken up the endeavor. In the leftist deep state narrative, the nemesis of the deep state was inherently the left (and increasingly the Kurds by the 1990s, in parallel with the rise of the PKK), the Islamist account twisted the narrative, depicting the archenemy of the deep state as Islam and its political outlets. Neither account was wrong, given the shift of the perceived threats after the end of the Cold War and the global rise of Islamism. In particular, the Gülen religious order became highly effective in disseminating the Islamist account, making it the most hegemonic in form. The Gülen movement was a religious community launched and led by retired cleric Fethullah Gülen (1942–) that gained huge political sway under the Islamist government by heavily infiltrating the bureaucracy and working in secret and that was later criminalized after a clash between the two. The brotherhood evoked a "moderate" Islamic view and was highly esteemed and envied for its well-trained and intellectually equipped devotees. Whereas the anti–deep state posture had a borne leftist tilt in the 1990s, deep state bashing became increasingly more predisposed to the progressive and democratic Islam allied with progressives and liberals who lambasted the autocratic and antidemocratic conduct of the bureaucratic tutelage in grabbing the democratic say of the people. Yet this new pro-democratic discourse was mainly a ploy of the Gülenists who were dominating the Islamic publishing sector, and, hence, the intellectual field, developing a new progressive Islamicate discourse blended with liberal vistas.

It became crystal clear that the Gülenists themselves had infiltrated the state's security bodies as part of a deliberate strategy that had been launched already by the 1980s, backed by center-right politicians seeking to engender a support base.[13] By the 2000s, Gülenists had become not only preeminent within the police and judiciary but also, more troublingly, in the military, long viewed as the secular bastion closed to any infiltration as the self-assured Turkish military known for paranoidly monitoring the military schools and cadets. The extent of the infiltration was so extensive that the Gülenists dared to attempt a coup in 2016 that failed severely. In short, by the 2010s, the Gülenists had themselves become "the deep state" while feigning to oppose it, manipulating the leftist and liberal intellectuals who had heartily supported them against Kemalist authoritarianism. This was a "conspiracy within a conspiracy".

In 2007, waves of arrests began that saw many military figures taken into custody for allegedly running a clandestine network. Soon, newspapers were running stories based on leaks from interrogations exposing a state-within-state organization "Ergenekon" (named after an epic from Turkish mythology) that included high-ranking generals, businesspeople, bureaucrats and former politicians that dominated behind the scenes in their respective fields. The probe was hailed by many leftists and liberals as the first overt exposure of the deep state and a coming to terms with the long-speculated deep state. The arrest of a number of high-ranking generals and police chiefs was celebrated by leftists and liberals, seeing it as a massive move toward Turkish democratization, holding many notorious figures accountable for their transgressions and haughtiness. Gülenist journalists such as Emre Uslu, Mehmet Baransu and Şamil Tayyar, among others, wrote extensively on "startling revelations" that were based mainly on leaks made by Gülenist prosecutors and police chiefs, many of which were, in fact, forgeries or manipulations.[14] This purported eradication of the deep state operation turned out to be a Gülenist plot run by Gülenist police, prosecutors and judges, aimed deliberately at pacifying those resisting the Gülenists' imposition of full power within the security establishment (with the support of the ruling Islamist AKP). What was branded as an elimination of the deep state turned out to be an incursion and an attempt to take over the state, corroborating the claims of those who had argued that Islamists were creating their own deep state and thus embarrassing liberal optimists.

In fact, the left's and liberals' whole-hearted espousal of the "deep state trials" displayed an idiosyncratic type of conspiratorialism: liberal conspiratorialism. Out of their deep distrust to Kemalist authoritarianism, nationalism and the military's preeminence and witnessing shady connections and political violence remaining undisclosed, they became easy prey to the deep state meta-narrative melding fiction with reality. They readily found "deep state" lurking behind every political development, operating schemes and designing the political order, business and media. Things are not what they seem! One needs to be watchful against the machinations of the deep state in the name of democracy, progress and liberal values! Deep state as a loosely defined concept and far-reaching elusive threat enthralled liberals. Liberals' and leftists' experiences, lifelong political struggles and commitments, sensibilities, agendas and convictions facilitated their seduction into this metanarrative. This tendency also stemmed partially from a certain historical interpretation of modern Turkey popularized among the revisionist left by the 1990s that attribute all the ills to the all-powerful Kemalist authoritarian state. This approach reduced the political conflict to a dichotomy between the mighty authoritarian state and civil society composed of the disenfranchised, including Kurds, Alevis and Muslims. As articulated earlier, this narrative was amplified by the Gülenist media outlets that touted leftists and liberals who championed this narrative. Whereas nationalism is deeply bent to conspiracy theories, "progressive" anti-nationalism also looks not immune to conspiratorial rhetoric.

Once the Gülenists clashed with the AKP in a bid to retain their bureaucratic power and further increase their clout, they were eradicated by the AKP after an atrocious showdown between the two. In the period that followed, criminalized Gülenism-bashing became the new source of CTs, and the Gülenist bureaucratic network came to be known as "the parallel state" that operated independently of the "official state".[15] The term *parallel state* was first used by Abdullah Öcalan, the imprisoned founder and leader of the PKK, when he accused Gülenist civil servants of taking orders, giving orders and interacting not based on bureaucratic hierarchy, but on the hierarchy within their own religious brotherhood, with Fethullah Gülen at the top. The Gülenist network was running a parallel organization within the state, and although the Gülenists were responsible for many outrageous offenses, they were blamed for many other things, becoming a scapegoat for the government in whitewashing its failures. The CTs revolving around Gülenists thus reached new levels of absurdity.

The deep state was, and is a fact, without question. Yet this alluring refrain has prompted a conspiratorial craze/industry in the hands of intellectual entrepreneurs. The "deep state" concept was exported from Turkey to the international arena, both as a serious analytic concept[16] and as a conspiratorial buzzword.[17] In the United States, the "deep state" became the mantra of far-right groups, pundits, tweeps and Internet forum and social media users. This was, however, not new ground for right-wing CTs who had long detected an overwhelming but underground liberal establishment in Washington, D.C., and New York that was in control of politics, the intellectual milieu and the arts. The CTs surrounding the Kennedy assassination all pointed to the prevalence of an imagined all-pervasive deep state. The concept was dubbed as the "establishment", the "military-industry complex" and the "dual state" (Ernst Fraenkel) in progressive and academic parlance. Furthermore, many other countries displayed even more overt "deep state" characteristics, such as Pakistan, where the notorious (especially in the eyes of US State Department and the military dealing with their Pakistani counterparts) military intelligence ISI possessed real power, running its conduct unfettered from the elected governments. In Greece, the Cold War security establishment as best monumentalized in Costa Gavras's movie *Z*, was named *parakratos* (para-state).[18] Deep state, however, seemed to be a better moniker explicating the machinations of the intransigently disguised structures of power, especially for the Donald Trump camp.

As a presidential candidate, Donald Trump accused the Obama government incessantly for transgressing democratic procedures and running a deep state. He has continued to tweet on the deep state during his presidency, claiming the Mueller probe was orchestrated by it. The "deep state revelations" of the anonymous, allegedly deep state insider known as "Q" (self-ascribed due to his purported Q clearance) on 4chan went viral and were followed by endorsements by conservative pundits such as Alex Jones, Jerome Corsi, Sean Hannity and others, with Q signs and T-shirts appearing later at Trump's rallies. The prolific right-wing conspiratorial pundit Jerome Corsi published a book titled *Killing the Deep State: The Fight to Save President Trump*, which opened with the statement "Donald Trump beat 16 Republican challengers and Hillary Rodham Clinton to win the presidency. Now he must beat the Deep State to keep his presidency. Here's how!"[19] This was followed by several other conservative conspiratorial books, all exposing the deep state controlling the FBI, CIA, NSA and judiciary and machinating against Trump. Another book, which was praised by Alex Jones on Infowars, claimed that "[t]he Deep State conspired to take down Trump. This book fills in all the details, and names names. All patriots need to read it".[20] Although Turkey remains a net CT importer, this is the small contribution of Turkish CT community and conspiracy theorists to the international CT epistemic community.

Turkey's missing John F. Kennedy–at–Dallas moment

Turkey's John F. Kennedy (JFK)–at–Dallas moment could be the killing of the then-president (ruling the country from 1983 to 1991 as prime minister, and then as president with limited presidential powers between 1991 and his death in 1993) Turgut Özal, if it had actually taken place. Many remained unconvinced that Özal (the diminutive, fat and the unhealthy president who had undergone extensive cardiovascular surgery and who had constantly dismissed the advice of doctors to lose his extra 30-plus kilograms to abandon his high-calorie diet ten years ago due to his weak heart condition) had died after a heart attack, suspecting he may have been poisoned. This was, indeed, a politically motivated and deliberately disseminated CT that flourished especially among the conservative audience.

Özal was an idiosyncratic politician who came from a conservative background, who was pious but also liberal, and who was a daring iconoclast, calling for the demolition of the security-obsessed culture of the state and ending up with all the ideologies in favor of a Fukuyaman end-of-history paradigm.[21] He was also controversial for other reasons, such as his relentless advocacy of unbounded free market ideology (a Thatcherite committed to TINA), using slang and obscene language ("Tell it to little Turgut", he once said, implying his sexual organ), his deriding his contestors as old-fashioned dinosaurs unable to understand the contemporary. He was loathed by many for his provocatively taboo-breaking musings, such as openly speculating over a federative state of Turks and Kurds, while for many he was a closet Islamist, concealing his real intentions, and for others a stooge of US imperialism. He was also seeking a peaceful resolution with PKK.[22]

The year of his death was a hectic one. A short-lived ceasefire with the PKK came to an end one month later after a massacre perpetrated by the PKK with unclear motivations and without an order from the top. Allegedly provoked by the atheist intellectual Aziz Nesin's translation project of the *Satanic Verses*, in Sivas, a conservative city, Islamists burned down a hotel in which he was staying while partaking a leftist event, causing the death of 34 people, many of them leftists. For many, there was a deliberate orchestration behind this seemingly spontaneous lynching and other ostensibly coincidental developments. For the conspiracy theorists, these incidents were all a ploy of the "deep state" that also killed Özal, aiming to obstruct the peace offensive gauging that its political clout was no more secure. By killing Özal, the deep state had arguably eliminated its main threat.[23]

The Gülenists were active in propagating and promoting this CT, being on close terms with Özal who was allied with them in his fight against his bureaucratic adversaries. For the Gülenists, Özal was their man – deeply religious, but also at home in the modern world playing the game according to the rules.[24] This was mostly distortion, selling a selective image of Özal to their cadres with an overexaggeration of their political influence. Hence, Özal's elimination amounted to a purported offensive against the Gülenist vision of Turkey that would soon be restored. The Gülenist cadres were overwhelmingly infatuated with this CT, and by the 2000s, as the Gülenists were becoming more powerful in politics and the media, giving them more sway in molding public opinion, this CT became disseminated widely among the conservative circles. Özal's widow and his son were given airtime to voice this CT, which his widow, in particular, believed to be clearly factual. It was first Gülenist media outlets that continuously speculated over this theme, and Özal's body was even exhumed for an autopsy, with Gülenist media outlets and, following them, Islamist media misleadingly maintaining that poison had finally been detected in his blood. One

Gülenist journalist, Aytekin Gezici, had published a thick volume entitled Who Killed Özal in which he purportedly revealed the autopsy in minute detail, a secret hidden from the public, proving conclusively the poisoning framing the official position of Gülenists.[25] After breaking with the Gülenists, the Islamists now blamed Gülenist doctors of obstructing and distorting Özal's autopsy in order to manipulate Erdoğan by delivering a falsified autopsy report.[26] This absurdity acknowledged the fabrication while the original claim was not recanted.

The death of Muhsin Yazıcıoğlu (1954–2009), who was the leader of a small right-wing party welded around his personal charisma with the tacit support of the Gülenists but with sufficient charisma to encompass the entire right-wing camp, whose helicopter crashed in forest lands in the snow while campaigning for the 2009 elections, also prompted a CT craze, led again by the Gülenists, who maintained command over the Islamic intellectual scene. A few weeks after his death, Baskın Oran, a highly respected socialist academic and intellectual stated that Yazıcıoğlu had asked to meet with him and other left-liberal intellectuals,[27] as an extraordinary feat, given Yazıcıoğlu's radical nationalist stance. Yazıcıoğlu was allegedly to speak of maneuverings over his party's youth branch, many of whom had been involved in politically motivated crimes. Yazıcıoğlu's death remains shrouded in mystery, and a bounty for conspiracy theorists, among whom Yazıcıoğlu espoused charisma and stature, despite his party's paltry presence. The purported murders of these two notable conservative politicians continued to be conducive in the propagation of a "deep state" fantasy serving the self-righteousness of the self-victimized political right.

Notes

1 "İşçi Kesimi Davasında On Beş Sanık Tahliye İsteminde Bulundu", *Cumhuriyet*, July 10, 1973; "Bomba Davası Sanığı Dr. Eren İddiaları Reddetti", *Cumhuriyet*, July 11, 1973; "İşçi Kesimi Davasında İki Sanık Daha Tahliye Edildi", *Cumhuriyet*, July 12, 1973; "256 Sanıklı Davada Emekli Subay Gümüştaş da İşkenceden Yakındı", *Cumhuriyet*, October 2, 1973.
2 "Bomba Olayları Davasında Bir Sanık Kontr-Gerilla'yı CIA'nın Kurdurduğunu Öne Sürdü", *Cumhuriyet*, October 17, 1973.
3 İlhan Selçuk, *Ziverbey Köşkü* (İstanbul: Çağdaş Yayınları, 1987) 63. Also see, Murat Yetkin, *Meraklısı İçin Casuslar Kitabı* (Istanbul: Doğan Kitap, 2018), 234–240.
4 Ecvet Kılıç, *Özel Harp Dairesi* (İstanbul: Turkuvaz Kitap, 2009), 161–164; Belma Akçura, *Derin Devlet Oldu Devlet* (İstanbul: New Age Yayınları, 2009), 27–29.
5 Daniele Ganser, *NATO's Secret Armies: Operation Gladio and Terrorism in Western Europe* (London: Routledge, 2004).
6 Mehtap Söyler, *The Turkish Deep State* (London, New York: Routledge, 2015).

7 Ryan Gingeras, *Heroin, Organized Crime & the Making of Modern Turkey* (New York: Oxford University Press, 2017).

8 Ertuğrul Özkök, "Derin Devlet Sözünün Mucidi", *Hürriyet*, November 25, 1997.

9 Uğur Mumcu, *Silah Kaçakçılığı ve Terör* (İstanbul: Tekin Yayınevi, 1981); Uğur Mumcu, *Papa-Mafya-Ağca* (İstanbul: Tekin Yayınevi, 1984).

10 Thomas Melley, *The Covert Space: Secrecy, Fiction, and the National Security State* (Ithaca; London: Cornell University Press, 2012), 35.

11 Ibid., 199–222.

12 For the series, see Volkan Yücel, *Kahramanın Yolculuğu: Mitik Erkeklik ve Suç Draması* (İstanbul: Bilgi Üniversitesi Yayınları, 2014).

13 Zübeyr Kındıra, *Fetullah Gülen'in Copları* (İstanbul: Su Yayınları, 2001); Hanefi Avcı, *Haliç'te Yaşayan Simonlar* (Ankara: Angora, 2010); Ahmet Şık, *Paralel Yürüdük Biz Bu Yollarda* (İstanbul: Postacı Yayınevi, 2014), 90–91.

14 Mehmet Baransu, *Karargah* (İstanbul: Karakutu, 2010); Mehmet Baransu, *Pirus: Devşirme Orduların Son Savaşı* (İstanbul: Karakutu, 2012); Emre Uslu, *Dün Kürtler Bugün Cemaatler* (İstanbul: Karakutu, 2010); Adem Yavuz Arslan, *Bi' Ermeni Var: Hrant Dink Operasyonun Şifreleri* (İstanbul: Timaş, 2011); Şamil Tayyar, *Operasyon: Ergenekon* (İstanbul: Timaş Yayınları, 2008); Şamil Tayyar, *Çelik Çekirdek: Türkiye'de Derin Devletin Tarihi* (İstanbul: Timaş Yayınları, 2010).

15 Ahmet Şık, *Paralel Yürüdük Biz Bu Yollarda*, 505–506.

16 For some journalistic perspectives, see David Remnick, "There Is No Deep State", *New Yorker*, March 20, 2017. www.newyorker.com/magazine/2017/03/20/there-is-no-deep-state; Marc Ambinder, D. B. Grady, *Deep State: Inside the Government Secrecy Industry* (Hoboken, NJ: John Wiley & Sons, 2013). Also see from an insider's perspective, see Mike Lofgren, *The Deep State* (New York: Penguin, 2016).

17 Nebojša Blanuša, "The Deep State Between the (Un)Warranted Conspiracy Theory and Structural Element of Political Regimes?" *Critique and Humanism*, 48(2), 2018, 63–82.

18 I thank Nikola Karasová for bringing *parakratos* to my attention.

19 Jerome Corsi, *Killing the Deep State* (West Palm Beach: Humanix Press, 2018), www.amazon.com/Killing-Deep-State-Fight-President/dp/1630061026.

20 Theodore Roosevelt Malloch, *The Plot to Destroy Trump: How the Deep State Fabricated the Russian Dossier to Subvert the President* (New York: Skyhorse Publishers, 2018).

21 For his views, see his book-length interview published posthumously, Mehmet Barlas, *Turgut Özal'ın Anıları* (İstanbul: Sabah Kitapları, 1996).

22 For Turgut Özal, and the controversies that surround, him, see Feride Acar, "Turgut Özal: Pious Agent of Liberal Transformation", in Metin Heper, Sabri Sayari (eds.), *Political Leaders and Democracy in Turkey* (Lanham: Lexington Books, 2002). For the Motherland Party of 1980s, see Ersin Kalaycıoğlu, "The Motherland Party", in Metin Heper, Barry Rubin (eds.), *Political Parties in Turkey* (London, Portland: Frank Cass, 2002). Also, for some insightful portraits of Özal, see Yavuz Gökmen, *Özal Sendromu* (Ankara: V Yayınları, 1992); Hasan Cemal, *Özal Hikayesi* (Ankara: Bilgi Yayınevi, 1989).

23 For the framing of this narrative on the part of conservative opinion leaders, see Hakkı Öznur, *1993: Örtülü Darbe* (İstanbul: Timaş Yayınları, 2012);

Şamil Tayyar, *Kıt'a Dur* (İstanbul: Timaş Yayınları, 2009); Zihni Çakır, *Korku İmparatorluğu Gladyo* (İstanbul: Profil Yayıncılık, 2009).

24 For example, see the account in Turgay Yavuz, *Özal'ın Mirası: Anılarıyla Ekrem Pakdemirli* (İstanbul: Timaş Yayınları, 2013).

25 "Özal'ın Otopsisi Bile Ortada Kalmış", *Yeni Şafak*, September 29, 2010; "Özal'ın Cenazesine Hassas Otopsi", *Yeni Şafak*, September 29, 2012; "Özal'ın Otopsi Tutanağında Şok Detay", *Sabah*, June 16, 2013.

26 "Ahmet Özal Tezgahı Deşifre Etti", *Takvim*, March 5, 2014.

27 Ali Bayramoğlu, "Muhsin Yazıcıoğlu Yazarlarla Neden Görüşmek İstedi?" *Yeni Şafak*, April 4, 2009.

5   Islamist conspiracy theories in power (2002–)

Even before the United States, it was the Middle East that was almost exclusively associated with conspiracy theories (CTs) as a geographical region. In an early survey of CTs in the Middle East, Daniel Pipes articulated the intrinsic propensity of Middle Easterners/Muslims to believe in absurdities of all sorts and, hence, CTs. His father, Polish *émigré* Richard Pipes (1923–2018), had been a fervent Cold Warrior who dedicated his life to fighting communists on the intellectual front as an eminent historian of Russia at Harvard University. Ironically, Pipes *fils* studied Islamic history as if seeing Islam a new threat to US national security. He would later become an "Islamic expert", exposing the "leftist and liberal subservience to Islamofascism", especially on campuses (via website Campuswatch), and penned an early study in this genre that was teeming with orientalism, seeing Muslims as naturally predisposed to CTs.[1] It is no secret that the Middle East is rampant with CTs, many of which also functioned as ideological outlets for dictatorships.[2] Yet in the post-9/11 conspiratorial universe that fueled paranoia in the West, one needs to consider proneness to CTs as a human tendency that became more exposed in certain political structures, cultures, ideological sets and discursive universes.

Probing the surging conspiratorial culture within the ruling Islamist AKP (Justice and Development Party), and its public intellectuals, this chapter examines Islamist CTs not as intrinsic Islamic proclivities but as political maneuvers used to attain other ends. After providing a brief outline of this conspiratorial universe, it examines the sources of the conspiratorial culture and mechanisms behind the establishment of absolute truths and absolute enemies.

The conspiratorial culture of the AKP and Islamist intelligentsia considers all perceived domestic and international foes to be allied in a deep collaboration. In the aftermath of the Arab Spring, domestic politics and foreign policy became inextricably intertwined in Turkey, and this shift birthed a new conspiratorial universe in which the domestic and the international could not be dissociated. Accordingly, all domestic opposition, including the Gezi protestors, leftists, Kemalists and the Kurdish movement, were to be framed as in an alliance with Zionists, neocons, Baathists and other dark forces.

Evidently, the inherited Islamist political discourse was deeply entrenched within a conspiratorial universe in which all modern history and international politics were perceived as part of the far-reaching struggle between those following the path of Allah and those committed to derailing them from their path. Yet Islam as an ideology and Islamism as a political technology in the service of a propagandist state are two different animals. Rather than explaining this conspiratorial culture as inherent in the Islamist mind, or as a reflection of the irrational mind, I put forward a more "political" explanation, arguing that the conspiratorial universe was promoted by Erdoğan to consolidate his one-man rule within the party and to establish a personality cult among his followers, delegitimizing any dissent among the party rank and file. Dissociating the party and its embedded intellectuals (or apparatchiks) from any ideology, including Islamism, through this maneuver, Erdoğan could wield his own cult and secure personalized loyalty, styling himself as the only man strong enough to stand up against the manifold fatal threats. This chapter provides a brief overview and assessment of this conspiratorial culture and the mechanisms that went into creating it.

Sacralization of politics and inventing enemies

The 1990s witnessed the rise of Islamism in Turkish politics. The Welfare Party, promoting an Islamist agenda, enjoyed an initial stunning 19% of the vote in the local elections in 1994, and added a further 2% to its support in the general elections the following year, emerged as the largest party with 21% of the vote.[3] The coalition established by the Welfare Party and the secular center-right True Path Party (TPP) would, however, be terminated in a de facto coup perpetrated by the military. Following the "postmodern coup", as it was dubbed by General Erol Özkasnak, secretary of the National Security Council and one of the leading protagonists of the "postmodern coup", Welfare Party chairman and prime minister Necmettin Erbakan was forced to resign and acquiesced to the founding of a new coalition government by secularist parties with the backing of the military.[4]

The Welfare Party was subsequently banned for its "anti-secularist activities",[5] and its successor, the Virtue Party, would meet a similar fate. This led the young reformist elements in the party to break away from the old guard and launch their own political venture. Critical of the traditional mosque-based politics of the old guard, the young reformists maintained that it was not enough to attract the pious with religious messages, stating that the party needed to have mass appeal. The AKP was founded in 2001 by those who had parted ways with the Islamist movement and looking to create a new party that followed the secular premises of the republic but with extensive and freer political space for the promotion of their conservative/Islamic political and cultural agenda. It was to be a "reformed Islamist" party, breaking away from Islamism's immediate political agenda but retaining and reinventing its cultural heritage and self-identity in different ways. The AKP endorsed an unprecedentedly bold liberal vision, advocating the broadening of democratic and civil rights, as stated in the party program, while providing intellectual references in support of its Islamist background and the conservative profile of its leadership and cadres.[6]

Yet, the AKP's reformism and enthusiasm for accession to the European Union waned, and the party would become increasingly authoritarian, shifting to populist discourses amalgamating populism with Islamism. The triumphalism subsequent to the elimination of military defiance rendered it more authoritarian than ever. Imposing its grip on power with the marginalization of the military by 2010, it was able to forsake its erstwhile semi-liberal attitudes, and distancing itself from its erstwhile liberal allies, the party fostered a homegrown Islamist intelligentsia as its need to hold onto a liberal rhetoric ceased. This intelligentsia promoted a conspiratorial culture that blended inherited Islamist discourses with conspiracy theories imported from the West in the age of CTs. Treating politics not as a game of pragmatic give-and-take but as an ultimate and perpetual struggle between good and evil, the AKP and its intellectual-academic complex drifted toward a conspiratorial culture that was, for sure, an extension and corollary to the brewing political and intellectual environment that was to come.

Not yet just another political party contesting for votes and seeking temporary political office via the ballot box, AKP projected itself as bearing a timeless and metaphysical ideal. With no difference observed among the ideals, the party and the state, this presumption brought in a trivialization of politics, being no longer a mediation of ideas among members of the polis in the public sphere with the goal of coming up with optimal policy guidelines and delivering consent. Politics, as deliberated by Aristoteles in ancient Greece or interpreted by Arendt and Habermas in the 20th century as a constant dialogue among citizens in an agora with no recipe for redemption (in an Oakeshottian sense) was, however, pointless for the ascendant Islamist intelligentsia. Politics as such was not only prosaic but also profane. Politics rather should be a means for a transcendental essence. Those who are not admitted into the realm of the New Turkey were henceforth rendered *metic* and posited outside the legitimate political community. This was because the state (of "New Turkey") was defined not based on a political contract but on ideological and even ontological (given that piety is also an expected norm) premises.

The Islamist intelligentsia invented a new political lexicon to support the sacralization of politics,[7] ushering in a political vocabulary that sharply distinguished between what it was referred to as "Old Turkey" and "New

Turkey".[8] While the "Old Turkey" stood for the Islamist version of the *ancien régime*, "New Turkey" became the unofficial honorific bestowed on the new regime resembling the symbolism laden in Salazar's *Estado Novo* or Vichy's *état Français*. Accordingly, all the perceived threats and offensives leveled against the state could be portrayed as targeting not only Turkey but specifically "New" Turkey and what it stood for as well. Successfully disassociating itself from the legacy of the predecessor governments, this discourse arrived at a point of selective statism in which nationhood was defined based not solely on ethnicity or nationality but also on ideological loyalty and conformity. The state was not a realpolitik entity but the bearer of transcendental and sacrosanct values and ethos, as in the case of "New Turkey".

In such a situation, enemies were legion, being both domestic and international, and apparent rival states are enemies, as in any other nationalist imagination. Although Turkey was not lacking in solid state-level enmities in the previous decades, the most notorious being Greece, globalization and the erosion of state power brought more treacherous and elusive enemies into view, some of which were superstate and some substate. In this conspiratorial universe, the "enemy" was not an agent one could easily identify but, rather, a diffuse, nebulous, obscure and omnipresent one. Furthermore, these singular enemies were depicted as derivations, puppets or agents of a mastermind. Although they may enjoy their own autonomy and own reasons and motivations, there prevails one omnipotent enemy with a capital *E*, as imagery that is best captured in the visions of the Protocols of the Elders of Zion and the earlier Counter-Enlightenment ur-text of modern CTs.

The "West", as discussed in previous chapters, is an abstraction that cannot be said to refer to an identifiable material reality. The "West" had been construed as the ultimate and irreconcilable enemy of the "we", whether this "we" referred to "Turks", "Muslims" or any amalgamation of these two partially overlapping, partially contesting identities. Yet the demonization of this elusive "West" was carried to new heights by the AKP. The ensuing emphasis on the "West" as an ontological entity was expedient for several reasons. The efforts of the nation-states to maximize their own national interests, including the super-mighty United States – as the common nemesis of all Third-World anti-imperialist nationalisms, leftists and Islamists – were seen as realpolitik exigencies. Yet the "West" – this unidentified and elusive entity – entertains no definite or visible material existence and hence entertains no tangible "national" interests. It implies an "idea" and an "ideal", and its interests are not material and political but super-political and even theological. Its enmity is ontological, and hence the nonmateriality of the purported West enhances the visions of this conspiratorial universe. The spotted adversaries within and without are bundled together as if they were extensions of one single and omnipotent master scheme.

Gezi protests: vulnerability amid claims of omnipotence

According to AKP intelluctuals, the enemies within not only are legion but are also constantly changing appearance while simultaneously remaining the same behind their facades. Initially, AKP propaganda drew a clearly defined dividing line between "the New Turkey" spearheaded by the AKP, and "the Old Turkey" dominated by the old guard, the Kemalist and secular military and the national security establishment. Another accompanying demonized categorization was the "White Turks" who were allegedly dominant in the "Old Turkey", resembling colonials in a tropical colony donning Panama hats. This was a label employed to stigmatize the secular and well-off upper-middle class, who were implicated as not rooted within society, and so -not sufficiently Turkish (hence "white", meaning more European looking than the average Turk), living in their urban secluded habitus, separated from the cultural and moral norms of society at large.[9] This discourse was further aggravated by the Gezi protests that broke out in 2013.[10]

The Gezi protests became the *beté noir* of the Islamist intelligentsia and their conspiratorial universe. Demonstrators had gathered initially to protest the planned building of a shopping mall on the site of Gezi Park at the very center of the city's bohemian quarter, yet what started out as a small-scale protest turned into a massive antigovernmental demonstration after the brutal police crackdown. Although starting out as an environmental protest with a minuscule following, the extreme police violence and the fact that the planned mall was part of a pet project of Erdoğan's to symbolically take over the prestigious and hip Beyoğlu, the hub of bohemia and entertainment, turned it into a hostile protest targeting exclusively Erdoğan and his cultural politics.[11] The protestors "occupied" the park for two weeks, stirring either great sympathy or hostility. Rising out of the counterculture and urban youth subculture and mocking the authorities with humor, the protestors had significant backing on social media, among whom were celebrities and intellectuals who celebrated the wit of the young protestors. The Gezi protests revealed that the robust political power wielded by the AKP and the Islamists hardly translated into cultural hegemony, a moral upper hand and esteem.

This failure and perceived vulnerability brought even more aggressive incursions against the media and civil society outlets, aiming to discredit them not only as enemies of the state but also of the nation.[12] Failing to attain the moral upper hand, it was the task of the AKP intelligentsia to frame the course of events in such a way that they would secure moral superiority and claims of legitimacy, against all odds. The most direct approach was to shift the debate from the Gezi protests and police brutality to the "big picture" that lay behind and implicated the Gezi protestors as unknowing or deliberate pawns in the service of global powers aiming to topple Erdoğan and to destabilize Turkey.[13]

Denying any agency to the protestors, the pro-government media lost no time in depicting them as on the payroll of foreign intelligence services. They claimed that the Gezi riots were masterminded as a part of a global conspiracy, although the resemblances drawn between the Tahrir and Gezi protestors were somewhat paradoxical, as the AKP had jubilantly endorsed the protests in Egypt and the fall of Mubarak. All of a sudden, an organization that was almost unheard of in Turkey was accused of being behind the Gezi protests – Otpor. Otpor, which became a household name overnight, was a Serbian youth association that had been instrumental in the ouster of Milosevic, supported by American state-financed nongovernmental organizations, such as the International Republican Institute (IRI) of the Republican Party and National Democratic Institute (NDI) of the Democratic Party.[14] The public also learned that Gezi protestors had been allegedly influenced and even trained by Gene Sharpe (1928–2018), an American academic and several-time Nobel Peace Prize nominee who had written extensively on means of nonviolent opposition and antigovernmental protests, encouraging them through his engagement. Sharpe was referred to in the writings of several Egyptian bloggers, who at the time of the Tahrir protests cited Sharpe and his writings as inspiration. George Soros was another household name who was blamed and became an object of disdain also for the Kemalists and leftists, being seen as working on behalf of neoliberalism and imperialism. "Civil society" (and the "open society" of Soros[15]) was thus seen in some circles as a smoke screen concealing subversive activities in the name of rights, liberties and democracy.[16]

A documentary was screened immediately after the Gezi protests on A Haber (A News) that revealed the murky origins of the riots. The documentary enumerated the "coloured" revolutions in "Georgia, Ukraine, Kyrgyzstan" as having been organized by Otpor, along with the Arab Spring. William Engdahl, an American fringe conspiratorial public intellectual who had written extensively on issues as varied as genetically modified organisms and the global energy business, appeared in the documentary as an expert on Otpor,[17] and the Otpor baton was picked up also by other TV programs on the pro-government media, such as the TV show *Sıradışı* (*The Outlier*), hosted by Turgay Güler. For Güler, "Otpor is an evangelical organization aiming to instil chaos until the Doomsday".[18] It was the random and meaningless reiterations of Güler's esoteric and conspiratorial buzzwords that carried his conspiratorial aura. Güler, who had previously written a couple of popular esoteric and conspiratorial novels (a substandard Dan Brown) before being recruited by the pro-government media, epitomized the archetype of an "conspiracy theory intellectual" whose vocabulary, imagination and terminology lie entirely within the confines of a conspiratorial universe in which any opinion that fell outside its boundaries was unheeded.

So why did the AKP's public intellectuals respond to the Gezi protestors with such a heavy load of CTs? One of the primary reasons why people or political collectivities turn to conspiracy theories is due to their failure and/or refusal to explicate multilayered and complex social developments, relations and trends that they abhor or renounce outright in a reasonable framework, so as not to justify them, while another motivation is to quash their moral panic. The Gezi protests were an apparently unforeseen antigovernmental outpouring, in terms of both their scale and fury, which presented a severe moral crisis to the Islamic intelligentsia. It is in the main lack of moral superiority and legitimacy that leads authoritarian regimes to subscribe to CTs, and in this context, they were led to stigmatize the protestors and dissidents as pawns of an overarching global order, hence transposing social chasms, cleavages and political divisions to the realm of international relations, geopolitics and international economics. Facing a moral crisis, the AKP and its public intellectuals subscribed readily to CTs, denying the protesters any moral agency or legitimacy.

This Manichean imagination conceived all the exigencies as bound to fall into one of the mutually exclusive camps. In this moral cosmology, no space for contingency is acknowledged, and whatever happens serves only one of the two camps – one bearing transcendental Good and the other Evil. Thus, any opposition to the Islamist government could and was inevitably conceived as being in the service of this overarching global plot.

The rise of cultural politics: LGBT and feminism as a Conspiracy

Although the AKP did not take an openly inimical stand against lesbian, gay, bisexual and transgender (LGBT) persons, and gay pride events had been peaceful and legal for more than a decade, LGBT activism became inescapably politically contested, beginning with the heavy and vocal presence of the LGBT community chanting and leading the Erdoğan slurs during the Gezi protests.[19] The eventual homophobic turn of the AKP came with a discourse that posited homosexuality as an artificial construct, fabricated to destroy family values and hence the mores and morals of Turkish/ Muslim society, thus weakening the national vigor. Although this homophobic dimension was never as central as Putin's discourse,[20] the idea that homosexuality was consciously promoted and politicized as a conspiracy took hold in journalistic pieces and on social media. Turkish state television (TRT) had halted participation in the Eurovision song contest by 2013, a national pastime since the 1970s, after investing heavily to win the contest for a second time since Sertap Erener's Eurovision victory in 2003. TRT chairman İbrahim Eren defended the decision, arguing that "[a]s a public broadcaster, I can't screen at 21:00 when children are around someone who sports [a] beard and wears a skirt . . . and who sees himself as neither a woman nor a man",[21] referring to Austrian Eurovision winner drag queen Conchita Wurst and the other queer Eurovision participants. For Eren, the Eurovision song contest had to stop being a carriage for the propaganda of "some" and return to its original format – as a song contest.

Obama's election to the US presidency boosted the dissemination of CTs. Whereas in the term of his predecessor George W. Bush, evangelical conspiracies were ubiquitously associated with the Bush administration and the neocon establishment, Obama's fifth column and agents of influence seemed to be homosexuals and the cultural left subculture. Feminism was another natural candidate for accusations of efforts to break the family unit that had been the bulwark against subversion, and the very base of the national community, diligently safeguarding the national mores. On the 2019 Women's Day, three weeks before the highly polarized municipal elections, to polarize the society as a pre-election scheme, not only the women's parade was banned but also the feminist activists were impugned for their glaring feminism and sexual politics. This denunciation benefited from stigmatization of feminism as an alien ideology seeking for an anti-national and subversive morality. Conspiracy theories were also raised showing feminism within the moral, cultural and ideological affinity of the "globalist" ideology." The aversion to Obama and the cultural-left themes in Turkey led the AKP intellectuals, apparatchiks and tweeps to enthusiastically support Donald Trump despite his downright Islamophobia who were overjoyed at Trump's astounding triumph in 2016. For the AKP opinion leaders and pundits, Hilary Clinton was the "establishment" and "globalist" incarnate, while Trump, in contrast, was "the man of the people", who, like Erdoğan, was challenging the establishment and the privileged.[22] It was no surprise that pro-Trump CTs like Pizzagate were so widely publicized in the Turkish pro-government media, revealing the hypocrisy of the Obamaites.[23] The passion of support for Trump was a demonstration of the immaculate coalescence of Islamist antiliberal discourse with the Western far-right (and increasingly alt-right) cultural and intellectual universe, despite the Islamophobia the Western right was fraught with.

Haşmet Babaoğlu, a left-liberal intellectual erstwhile known for his romantic takes but became an avid apologist of AKP, emerged as an extravagant interlocutor of fringe Western conspiratorialism addressing his newly found Islamic audience and Islamist intelligentsia. In his writings (and more blatantly and passionately in his tweets), he consistently unmasked the "myths of modern science" and challenged the "scientific order" on world's real age, world population, human prehistory and exposed other hoaxes (such as the moon landing and space explorations).[24] Babaoğlu's pursuits displayed the interwoven nature of the universes of Islamic conspiratorialism and

Western pseudoscience canon. Although Babaoğlu's stimuli stemmed from Western pseudo-science literature (and himself feigning to invoke reason against "modernist dogmatism and fanaticism"[25]), such "liberal" scientific order bashing captivated his Islamic audience. The Islamic counterscientific rhetoric also came to refute "Darwinism" (as if an ideology) as atheistic and materialistic dogma/pseudo-science benefiting from postmodern skepticism towards science.[26] In this hybrid discourse articulated by many Islamic intellectuals, feminism, "LGBT (lavender) lobby" and Islamophobia were all depicted as extensions of the hegemonic modernist and Eurocentric epistemology imposing itself as the sole and indisputable scientific truth. This scheme echoes the Republican portrayals of the liberals, academia, identity politics and gender activism in the United States.

CTs as state project: Pelicans, social media intimidation and beyond

Terms such as *communication* and *public diplomacy* became watchwords for the Islamist government. State bodies assigned to conduct "public diplomacy", while generous funds were channelled into quangos to defend and uphold the "Turkish position" vis-à-vis foreign public decision-makers and public intellectuals. However, state-authorized pundits, organized and paid for by the quangos and state bodies, when visiting European capitals, Washington, D.C., and New York, were to speak to audiences of five to ten, many of whom happened to be Turkish and affiliated with the government! The real communications strategy was, however, to generate, rear and disseminate CTs via media outlets, social media, state-affiliated facilities and quangos.

This strategy had become much more brazen by the mid-2010s, epitomized most blatantly by a network known somewhat ominously as "The Pelicans". The curious name came from an anonymous manifesto posted on WordPress on May 2016 titled conspicuously "The Pelican Brief" after the John Grisham novel and Alan Pakula movie, for no sensible reason, that accused the then–prime minister Ahmet Davutoğlu of conspiring against Erdoğan behind the doors, prompting his ouster from the prime ministry in just three days.[27] Although there were no names under the document, the collective authors behind the lines were immediately and unmistakably recognizable.

Although the generic name Pelican was coined immediately after this manifesto, the implicated circle was a network organized around a think tank (or a quango) with the corporate and professional-sounding name "Bosphorus Global", based in a lavish villa on the Bosphorus as berated by the victims of the manifesto.[28] The unit operated as an intellectual thug, galvanizing intellectual terror, with the main mission being to discredit and defame AKP and Islamist heavyweights with the potential to pose a threat to Erdoğan's grip of power. Launching a web portal (www.duvardibi.tv), they systematically accused Islamists and AKP insiders of inventing conspiracies. The fact that these heavyweight public intellectuals, journalists or ex-politicians were exercising authority and influence over the conservative constituency, political class and networks deemed them not only potentially more destabilizing and disquieting but also harder to discredit on ideological grounds. They were accused of being Trojan horses, fifth columnists, traitors to the Islamic cause and defectors (e.g., ex-AKP heavyweight Bülent Arınç was referred to as Lawrence of Manisa, after his hometown and the Lawrence of Arabia figure) for allegedly and secretly cooperating with enemies within and without. Liberals were not only dumped by Erdoğan but also impugned for perniciously tempting the conservative novices. Within this atmosphere, liaisons and affinities with liberals among the conservatives became suspect and were considered tantamount to heresy, backdoor dealing and treason. Consequently, the liberals, their copycat Islamist stooges and enthusiasts among the conservatives were easy prey for the carnivorous Pelicans.

Abdullah Gül, the ex-president of Turkey (2007–2014) and hitherto coequal partner of Erdoğan, was shrewdly marginalized over several years through incessant slanders depicting him as an agent of the "deep British state" purportedly proved by a variety of evidence. The smear campaign against Davutoğlu on social media, on the other hand, began while he was still serving as the prime minister (2014–2016), with accusations that he was conspiring against Erdoğan behind closed doors as a lackey of the international global elite, and the slurs continued even after his dismissal. One item of "evidence" of his betrayal was his education in the prestigious German-instruction high school IEL (İstanbul High School for Boys).[29] He was accused of being "pro-German" due simply to his educational background. The fact that the then–undersecretary of the foreign ministry and a key decision-maker with a staunchly secular background was another graduate of the school further "proved" the case. More conspicuously, Davutoğlu's undergraduate and graduate degrees from Bosphorus University, where instruction was in English and which was originally a US missionary boarding school, made him even more suspect. He was easily marked as a stooge of the Anglo-American global elite, having been trained in their very ideological garrison and even speaking the language seemed to be an adequate cause of suspicion. Erdoğan, on the other hand, speaks no foreign language, making him bulletproof against compromise.

Davutoğlu was no less Islamist than Erdoğan, yet he was resolute in imposing his own agenda. In fact, the overambitious Davutoğlu sought room to pursue his own politics and implant his cadres in the decision-making bodies in an attempt weaken Erdoğan's base in the government, for which he was made to pay dearly by means of humiliation. Those who defended him remained ineffective, meager and out of reach of the media and public, and Davutoğlu's purge was accompanied with the ouster of intellectuals (journalists, academics, etc.) who supported him as an alternative to Erdoğan's way of governance – some out of Islamist convictions, some for their moderate and semi-liberal convictions. All were pronounced unreliable and were systematically purged through social media as plotters against Erdoğan in collaboration with the global conspiracy. Operation Davutoğlu would be the Pelicans' masterpiece and perfect storm, through which they terrified the Islamic circles with shock and awe.

The Pelicans were funded generously by shady money channeled from state funds, running a sizable social media operation for the effective dissemination of CTs. These social media accounts, as well as journalists, academics and public figures affiliated with the network, promoted CTs to defame opposition of all kinds while also making preemptive strikes against potential threats. A constellation of journalists, academics, Twitter opinion leaders and trolls made up this network, contributing by acting, tweeting and retweeting, and the Pelicans remain notorious for their shameless defaming and disseminating of CTs to this end.

It was not long ago that cyberspace and social media were being hailed as free spaces, impervious to governmental intrusion and a bastion of free speech. Yet seeing social media and cyberspace as new areas for surveillance, states began developing means of policing them, with great effect, and turning cyberspace into a milieu of Orwellian newspeak.[30] The pinnacle of state social media manipulation is surely Russia, where trolls work as state employees 24/7 in comfortable offices.[31] In Turkey, state-funded or state-sponsored trolls (to be joined by volunteering partisan trolls) also devise CTs effectively to slander alternative views and groups through invention, promotion and dissemination through Internet memes and infographics.

Foreign policy front and CTs

The AKP enacted a highly activist and overambitious foreign policy in the Middle East. Arguing that, fraught with Kemalist inferiority complex, preceding governments had consciously neglected the Middle East as a means of dissociating Turkey from its Islamic roots, the AKP intelligentsia heralded in the dawn of regional cooperation and integration. Following the fall of Ben Ali in Tunisia followed by Mubarak in Egypt, the AKP intelligentsia hailed the course of events as an inevitable shift in the region towards Islamic solidarity. Yet things turned nasty. Syria became a hotbed for violent infighting between jihadists, Assad and his allies and others. More obnoxiously, with Assad's strategical support, the Democratic Union Party (PYD), as the Kurdistan Worker's Party's (PKK's) Syrian counterpart, took over political and military control of Syria's Kurdish-majority region, with this PKK control of the Turkish–

Syrian border causing yet another hurdle in the way of Erdoğan and Davutoğlu's overambitious dreams.

These failures ensued a wave of attacks against domestic foes accusing them of taking sides with the enemies abroad. By alleging that the opposition had collaborated with international enemies in a variety of ways, the AKP sought to gain the moral upper hand. The government's overambitious Islamic agenda and its ideologization of foreign policy stirred up the opposition, with both sides accusing each other of treachery. Foreign policy thus became an extension of domestic politics and cultural politics, creating both a political and an ideological divide. Islamist intellectuals consequently turned to CTs that allegedly revealed the hypocrisy of the opposition by linking them with Turkey's enemies, delineating impossible alliances and depicting domestic opponents as in collaboration with international foes.

The Middle East theater was also used to "export" righteousness and a rhetoric of victimhood. Auspiciously, just one month after the outbreak of the Gezi protests and the enjoyment of the moral high ground by the protestors, the military in Egypt toppled the Muslim Brotherhood (MB) government after a series of anti-MB protests in Tahrir Square led by the Tamarod movement, hence serving to justify the military coup. Portraying the Egyptian military as the bastion of secularism and associating it with the now politically moribund Turkish military, the AKP leadership used this attribution to discredit the Gezi protestors. Implying guilt by association, this linkage implied that Gezi protestors were coup mongers, pro-militarist and antidemocratic, like their protesting Egyptian brethren, in direct contradiction to their self-styling as peaceful, progressive and democratic demonstrators.[32]

As the Arab Spring was challenging and overthrowing Baathist and secular (and some left-leaning) dictatorships and the MB was on the rise, the dichotomy between the Baathist dictatorships and the MB was rendered absolute, overlooking the other popular grievances that had brought the protestors and other political contesters onto the streets, and consequently this dichotomy was subsequently applied/exported to the Turkish setting.[33] The MB was equated with the democratic aspirations of the masses, and hence the "national will" (*milli irade*), mirroring the AKP's self-portrayal as the political body of the "national will" and the Turkish people (as an organic community), organized against the usurper secular elite: "We have seen the true face and spirit of those who had praised the 'spirit of Gezi' and had delivered sociological justifications in the case of Egypt. Setting aside the scant genuine environmentalists of Gezi, what remains is an outright *coup d'etat*-mongering temper".[34]

Thus, the political divide, vocabulary and themes in Turkey were expanded to the Middle East. The AKP associated (and demonized) her domestic foes with her international foes, delineating an axis of evil that comprised such international foes such as Assad, Israel and Iran and domestic foes such as the secular opposition party RPP, the Gezi protestors and the Gülen religious brotherhood, depicting them in close collaboration and accusing them of running a conspiracy. The seculars were equated with the Baathists and Middle Eastern dictatorships: "We have a fight with the *baltagiya* in Egypt, with the *shabihas* in Syria, with the sectarians in Iraq and with the pro-Gezi people, Gülenists and Kobanists in Turkey".[35] In contrast, AKP was amalgamated into a transnational network with common sensitivities, agendas and destinies.[36] As the AKP promoted itself as an ardent backer of the street protests in the Middle East, they associated their domestic foes with the stalwarts of the dictatorships from Egypt to Tunisia and from Yemen to Syria. Hence, the national divide between the alleged "national will/nation" and the so-called secular elite was projected onto the Middle East and was sought to be justified within regional controversies and rifts. Kemal Öztürk (Ali Nur Kutlu), who had headed the state news agency AA, railed that

> [w]e don't keep cats or dogs; we don't cry for seals; we don't campaign for the rights of homosexuals. Instead, we raise pious children at home; we cry for our deceased Syrian brethren and campaign for the 528 innocents sentenced to death [in Egypt].[37]

Contrasting the actual sufferings of the Middle East with the snobbery of the Gezi protestors, whose agenda and priorities (like queer, animal rights and sexual freedom), Öztürk ridiculed the shallowness of their demands, accusing them of being out of touch with the people and reality. The Islamic democratization (Islamization and democratization seen as almost identical and complementing each other) of Turkey and the imminent democratization within the broader region were amalgamated in terms of not only the proponents but also the foes.[38] Thus, although their only common attribute was their animosity towards the AKP for disparate reasons, they were imagined as being in close cooperation masterminded by an international scheme. The prevailing ur-text and the Islamist counternarrative (as discussed extensively in the second chapter) was appropriated and updated in the geopolitics of the 2010s.

Historicization in the search for legitimacy and history as a conspiracy

The AKP's sacralization of politics was to be legitimized on historical grounds following the major shift of the Turkish Islamists' perceptions of the state. Long mistrustful of the state, seeing it as an apparatus of repression, in the 2000s, the Islamists were able to accommodate the liberal aversion to the state and authority through their Islamic proclivities. Yet subsequent to taking over the state, it did not take long for them to endorse the intransigent statist culture. This new identification was not that difficult, as they could now relate the Turkish state in its descent from Ottoman and Islamic polities and its transmission of the Turco-Islamic ethos ingrained with Islamic mores and ideals. Yet, this new state fetishism came with some novelties. Rather than incorporating the AKP government into the age-old transcendental Turco-Islamic culture of statehood and its ethos, this "New Turkey" was not a transcendental one but, rather, "our own state". The Islamist intelligentsia equated the state not only with the "party" but also with the ideals the party supposedly stood for and fostered. This historicization was couched in a conspiratorial consumption of history as a means of legitimacy building.

In 2017, TRT began to air a new TV series titled *Istanbul, the Capital* (*Payitaht İstanbul*) – a biographical drama of Abdülhamid II and his deeds during his long reign. The series was badly produced, even for TRT's usually low standards, but was announced with fanfare, heralding the extent of the significance attributed to production as a part of the ideological indoctrination. The representation of Abdülhamid II was revealing. The viewers were introduced to the court of the sultan, full of imbecilic, oblivious pashas who were so easily manipulated, deceived and compromised by the enemies of the empire, and more troublingly, it was Abdülhamid II alone who resisted this encroachment (see Figure 5.1). This imagery of Abdülhamid II was an obvious allegory of Erdoğan, who was also extolled and marketed as being in a permanent and daring fight against the enemies within and without,

Figure 5.1 TV series *Istanbul, the Capital* as Hamidomania. Abdülhamid II is constantly shown sitting on his throne as a symbol of authority depicted as self-assured, resolute, calm, perceptive and extremely well informed amid pervasive conspiracies against the empire in contrast to his grotesquely distraught and ill-advised entourage and pashas.

despite the mediocrity, timidity and even treachery of those closest to him and the state bureaucracy. In fact, the posture of the sultan was more ruffian rather than radiant with an imperial aura, which was an effort to associate Abdülhamid with Erdoğan, being rowdy in temper, posture, style and attitude.[39]

In one curious episode, the sultan slams the British ambassador, demonstrating his physical toughness when faced with an insult to national dignity, as another allusion to the very contemporary. Modern-day courses of events were reflected in the series, historicizing the present-day agendas, ideologies, proclivities and hostilities. The series was not timid in relating contemporary as the very last-minute political developments are brazenly incorporated into the series week by week. The anti-Erdoğan protestors, international financial plots to destabilize the economy and the unreliables within the bureaucracy were all projected into the reign of the sultan. The series was highly anti-Semitic – Herzl and the Zionism theme being a preeminent refrain, echoing the Islamist-conservative narrative formulated as conveyed and summarized in Chapter 2.[40] Carasso was also given a role, incredibly as contesting Herzl to lead the Zionist movement and become the "father of Zionism" but failed by only one vote.[41] The Rothschild family, as one of the financial backers and supporters of Zionism, also appeared in the series, eschewing the fact that Abdülhamid had allowed the Rothschilds to open a farm beside the other lands sold to the colonist Jews.[42] The series obviously sought to establish a direct link between the present day and the reign of Abdülhamid, showing that nothing has actually changed aside from some cosmetic alterations, with the enemies and their strategies remaining the same, thus justifying Erdoğan's current politics, discourses and fury. Not surprisingly, Erdoğan several times advised youth to watch the series "to learn their history" and the present as a reflection of history.[43]

The collapse of the Ottoman Empire entered the picture, historicizing the present-day antagonisms, locating them within a continuum and incorporating them into a larger and historical scheme. In 2016, as the centennial of the notorious Sykes–Picot treaty (the secret treaty concluded between Britain and France partitioning the Ottoman territories in the event of an Allied victory) was revoked from distant memory, becoming the ultimate symbol of Western intrusions into the Middle East, as well as the sinister and conspiratorial scheming of the Western powers.[44] Sykes–Picot was marked as responsible for the misery of the region, and the centennial also auspiciously coincided with the purported looming natural death of the treaty as the Middle East started to tear off the shackles imposed by the imperialist West. The people of the Middle East were taking their fate into their own hands, demonstrating in the streets and voicing their resentment. The artificial borders drawn up by the secret Sykes–Picot deal between Britain and France were on the verge of collapse, with the Middle East regaining its sovereignty. The Sykes–Picot theme was a godsend to those bombastically trumpeting the return of Turkey to the Middle East after a century of oblivion, subsequent to its disengagement from a region devised through imperialist scheming. Davutoğlu, who was at the time still prime minister, argued that

> [w]hen we look at the map [drawn at Sykes–Picot], we immediately fathom the objectives of the underlying mentality lurking behind the agreement: to tear Anatolia from Mesopotamia, to tear the Tigris and Euphrates from [the western Anatolian river of] Sakarya; to isolate the spirit of Mesopotamia from the spirit of Roumelia and Caucasia.[45]

Yet, one century later, things seemed to have changed. Although Turkey was resuscitated after decades of isolation with the coming to power of the AKP, the Middle East as a whole was simultaneously undergoing an era of rejuvenation, breaking off the shackles of Sykes–Picot that had "imposed the imperialist tutelage" over its peoples. This was not merely a coincidence, as the fortunes of Turkey and the Middle East are inextricably amalgamated, and it is no coincidence that their prospects thrive simultaneously. The Sykes–Picot theme also enabled the essentialization and historicization of the AKP narrative.[46]

Another "timely" and extremely expedient centennial celebrated with fanfare is the First Battle of Kut, fought during World War I in what is today southern Iraq and in which the Ottoman army defeated the British troops and took the British commander General Charles Townshend hostage. A pseudo-historiography of the commemoration of the battle was devised that claimed that the battle had been deliberately obliterated from history to erase the Turkish link to the Middle East by obscuring Ottoman victories by either (a) the Kemalist regime or (b) conceding to a British request following Turkey's accession to the North Atlantic Treaty Organization.[47] Davutoğlu, the then prime minister, argued at an event commemorating the battle, that "The Battle of Kut is not a victory that deserves obliteration. Yet, the Old Turkey mentality (*eski Türkiye anlayışı*) was for years shunned from evoking this battle, and even to thoroughly erase its memory".[48] The aforementioned *Derin Tarih* (*Deep History*), a popular Islamist historical magazine, devoted one of its cover issues to the battle, consecrating it as an obscured Ottoman victory.[49] The battle was also incorporated into the new school curriculum, with due space allotted by the Ministry of Education in 2017.[50] The state channel also screened a TV series on the heroism of the battle, curiously eulogizing the hero commander of the battle Halil (Kut) Pasha, who avenged Abdülhamid. Yet such inconsistencies are seen as trivial and poses no contradiction in the nationalist imagery which imagines a harmonious national past and pantheon of national heroes. History is employed to justify the present, and to relay present-day developments to historical inevitability and path dependency.

Erdoğan also referred recurrently to history to eternalize and historicize his politics and enmities. Historical legitimacy always serves as a trump card in the resolution of all immediate quandaries, contradictions and shortcomings. Identity politics also require a historical narrative that establishes absolute and irreconcilable nemeses that remain unchanged over time. The historical imagery couched in CTs suits such an agenda perfectly.[51] In November 2014, Erdoğan became a half-day sensation in the international media when he delivered a speech at the "Latin American Muslim Leaders Conference", organized by the Presidency of Religious Affairs of the Turkish state. According to Erdoğan, the myth buster, it was, in fact, Muslims who had "conquered" the Americas, which was a secret that was hidden so well so as to not give the Muslims due credit. Giving the date of this undercover expedition unmistakably as 1178, he provided evidence from the apocryphal memoirs attributed to Christopher Columbus.[52] Mistranslating the text in which the tops of the hills were likened to mosques as if a genuine mosque was implied, he delivered his conclusive evidence. Not unexpectedly, Erdoğan's eccentrics were immediately backed and further proved right by government mouthpieces.[53] In fact, the alleged Muslim discovery of the Americas had been prevailing within minor eccentric circles, and had been popularized especially by a certain Youssef Mroueh, a Lebanese immigrant to Canada, in short piece published by the "As-Sunnah Foundation of America".[54] Abdurrahman Dilipak, a Turkish Islamist public intellectual had also published a book on the "Muslim Discovery of America" back in 1984,[55] yet the theme was absurd and unheard of for the mainstream Muslim audience. This marginal CT was not only transmitted to the mainstream but also amplified and authorized. It was forgotten a few months later after instigating a heated public controversy and serving its function as all such indiscriminate historical revisionisms do.

Erdoğan's alternative takes on history were not limited to this speech. The international press loves to trumpet the periodic and recurring bravado of the preaching Erdoğan, airing them with sarcastic and bombastic commentary, including not only Erdoğan's conspiratorial and anti-Zionist bashings but also his eccentric historical revisionism. Erdoğan was subject to another round of bombastic international coverage when he installed a phalange of ceremonial guards dressed in the warrior costumes of the alleged 16 Turkish states founded throughout history.[56] The very awkwardness and outlandishness of the *mise-en-scéne* of Erdoğan posing with poorly tailored "warriors", dressed as if they had jumped out of PC games or an episode of *Game of Thrones*, ensured his domestic and international adversaries to enjoy a heyday. The spendthrift annual commemorations of the "conquest of Istanbul" just one week prior to the 2015 elections were a further subject of ridicule. His praise of the golden age of Islam, and his claims that Europeans had learned philosophy and science from the Muslims provided further opportunities to debunk not only him but also the "Islamist mind" in general.[57]

Apparently, it is not only the international media that poke fun at this bravado and historical revisionism, as such derision has been shown also by his opponents in Turkey who love to ridicule him at any given chance, not only to demonstrate his intellectual idiocy but also those of his constituency and his intellectual apparatchiks. Yet whenever his diehard adversaries enjoy a heyday, his other foes immediately rise, purportedly to outsmart their comrades, surmising that these erratic commentaries are, in fact, masterful political maneuvers handled by a political genius and criticize those who are more than willing to play his game.

Neither a political genius nor an oblivious demagogue, like Isaiah Berlin's hedgehog who knows one big thing, Erdoğan arguably plays the game he knows best: making provocative statements and, in doing so, leading and molding the political debate and lexicon, not unlike the Republican pundits love to do in the United States. Although Erdoğan uses incidental historical references for immediate political gain, the same strategy is employed constantly also by the Islamist intelligentsia and so cannot be reduced to political opportunism and propaganda. Historical revisionism is a constitutive part of Islamic public discourse, with historical references being an extremely convenient means of positing contemporary disputes in a larger context, creating justifications based on historical groundings that trivialize contemporary disputes and essentializing injustices and righteousness. For this, history needs to be rendered not as a patch of singular episodes but a grand theater of one overarching scheme.

A documentary screened in 2015 on the AKP outlet news channel A Haber (A-News) titled *The Mastermind* or, in more literal translation, *The Super-Mind* (*Üstakıl*) was an effort in that direction. The phrase was repeatedly articulated by Erdoğan in his claims that the plots against him were orchestrated by an elusive Supermind, and in one such speech, he challenged intellectuals, academics and journalists to expound more deeply on this Supermind. The two-hour documentary, which begins with Erdoğan heartily delivering this speech, argues that world history is, in fact, a sequence of incessant machinations of the Supermind, aimed at thoroughly dominating the world.[58] Every episode passed through in the world in history has been, in fact, another staging of this crusade. The good news, however, is that every offensive of the Supermind has been contested with a counterforce, resisting and challenging these machinations – "Abraham against Nimrud, Moses against the pharaoh" the voiceover maintains. World history was hitherto the eternal Manichean showdown between the Supermind (evil) and those who resisted it in the name the "eternal good", whether that eternal good be secular or theological.

After a brief prologue, the documentary reverts to the "Middle East, some 3,000 years ago" with an enigmatic melody playing in the background that is reminiscent of Peter Gabriel's *Passion*. We open on a vast desert with men in turbans, as a prototypical orientalist and anti-Semitic rendering of the ancient Jews, although the documentary is careful not to be depicted as anti-Semitic. The voice-over immediately reminded that those who were in the service of the Supermind were not Jews, per se, as true Jews were devout believers. It was the Jews who had parted from the path of Moses and who sought earthly vanity who were implicated in the plotting conspiracies. According to the documentary, Hitler was yet another accomplice of the Supermind. The documentary ends in the present day as we learn that the New Turkey of Erdoğan is the primary target of the Supermind, being the greatest threat to its road to power. At the close of the documentary, the question is asked, "Where lies the Supermind?" It would seem to be like the specter of communism that haunts Europe – being simultaneously everywhere and nowhere. One needs to be attentive to identify the next incursion of the Supermind, as it may come in many unlikely disguises, appearing in the form of ISIS (the Islamic State of Iraq and Syria), the PKK, seemingly innocent environmental protestors or a financial oligarchy. This documentary secularized the Islamist narrative without openly claiming Islamic justification but unquestionably implying an Islamic agenda inventing an absurdity as arcane as the Elders of Zion. Murat Akan, a pro-government journalist and entrepreneuring conspiracy theorist published this historical account in book form conveying world history and modern Turkish history adapted to the Supermind narrative. Such conspiratorial buzzwords allowed intellectual entrepreneurs to capitalize on them for fame, money, publicity and career prospects as well as an opportunity to further prove their loyalty and subservience.[59]

Conclusion: CTs to build politics of eternity

What were the reasons for this drift toward conspiratorial thinking? The conspiratorial tilt of Islamism is no secret, as Turkish Islamism, as had been the case with any other form of Islamism in the world, had been saturated with conspiratorial instincts in which the Jews, Zionists and Freemasons dominated, or sought to dominate, the world. The Protocols of the Elders of Zion had been the quintessential ur-text of this conspiratorial mind that had been slightly appropriated for Islamist predilections since its earliest translations and dissemination throughout the Islamic world.[60] The duality and the preordained encounter between the imperialist and infidel West and the beleaguered Islamic world dictate the tenor of the Islamist imagination. Yet, although the continuities with the Islamist mind are obvious, several twists and diversions are readily apparent. First and foremost, although Islamism had existed as an ideology with rigid and inflexible preconceptions and dictums, the new conspiratorial universe of the AKP is designed, somewhat haphazardly and mercurially, around a single man: Recep Tayyip Erdoğan. A major motivation behind the boosting of CTs by the pro-government media was, in fact, the establishment of the one-manship of Erdoğan.

It was no accident that the pro-government media gravitated toward a conspiratorial vision that coincided with Erdoğan's imposition of his personalized power, sidelining and marginalizing such AKP stalwarts as the then-president Abdullah Gül (and then Davutoğlu), hence destroying the intraparty consultative decision-making practice. The AKP thus transformed into a nonparty, organized as a leader–cult platform, after once being ideologically flexible, pragmatically liberal, conservative and Islamist. The invention of enemies both within and without required the vigilance and toughness of a strong leader (like Putin) and evidently served the personal agenda of Erdoğan, and CTs were highly effective in underpinning this political maneuver.

Authoritarian politics need enemies if legitimacy is to be produced and reproduced. Furthermore, as ideologies wane, they seek unidentified, elusive and metaphysical enemies rather than concrete ones such as stigmatized alternate ideologies and political movements. Turkish Islamism had been a rock-solid ideology with an absent-minded but definite agenda, passions and visions, although that rock-solid ideology was certainly fraught with conspiratorial culture, anti-Semitism and historical fiction. Yet, commitment, conviction and intellectual claims constitute the tenor of any given political ideology. By removing any opinion or ideal from the party and its affiliated intellectual elite, whether liberal or Islamist, Erdoğan enforced not only an ideological commitment and zeal but also an unconditional allegiance to his personalized rule. To uphold subservience, he needed enemies whose hostilities were not mundane or grounded on a conjectural realpolitik or national interests but, rather, on an ontological grounding.

This political technology was defined by Timothy Snyder as "politics of eternity" (as opposed to mundane politics) in his analysis of Putin and his strategists,[61] and he further observed that "politics of doing" had been replaced by "politics of being" (fixed – national, religious, cultural – identities), couched in the politics of eternity.[62] Putin's political technologists employed CTs as a means of effectively fortifying Putinism, while his archpolitical technologist Vladimir Surkov deployed them to formulate and foster his concept of "sovereign democracy". Through this approach, all enmities were rendered moral, ontological and perpetual, ensuring the vanishing of the "political".[63] The historicization of CTs further trivialized "today", deeming it ephemeral in the eternal grand theater of history and struggles, and this historicization also trivialized transient moral transgressions. As wars render morality a secondary concern that needs to be reassessed within the reality of war while also justifying misdemeanors, the introduction of history as a theater depicting a perpetual state of war also deems moral claims inconsequential and petty in the larger theater of history. CTs remain as an effective means of depoliticizing public debate and imposing the politics of eternity, having served these ends succinctly in Turkey.

Notes

1 Daniel Pipes, *The Hidden Hand: Middle East Fears of Conspiracy* (New York: St. Martin's Press, 1996).
2 Matthew Grey, *Conspiracy Theories in the Arab World* (London: Routledge, 2010); David Cook, *Contemporary Apocalyptic Literature* (Syracuse: Syracuse University Press, 2005).
3 For the rise of Welfare Party, see Hakan Yavuz, "Political Islam and the Welfare (Refah) Party in Turkey", *Comparative Politics*, 30(1), 1997, 63–82. Also see Haldun Gülalp, "Globalization and Political Islam: The Social Bases of Turkey's Welfare Party", *International Journal of Middle East Studies*, 33(3), 2001, 433–448; Ziya Öniş, "The Political Economy of Islamic Resurgence in Turkey: The Rise of the Welfare Party in Perspective", *Third World Quarterly*, 18(4) 1997, 743–766.
4 For Welfare Party's policies and dispositions in power, see Jenny White, "Pragmatists or Ideologues? Turkeys Welfare Party in Power", *Current History*, 96, 1997, 25–30.
5 For the published text of the public attorney's bill of indictment demanding the banning of the Welfare Party, see *Refah Partisi Kapatma Davası* (İstanbul: Kaynak Yayınları, 1998).
6 For some academic assessments of AKP, see William Hale, "Christian Democracy and the AKP", *Turkish Studies*, 6(2), 2005, 293–310; İhsan Dağı, "Transformation of Islamic Identity in Turkey", *Turkish Studies*, 6(1), 2005, 21–37. Fulya Atacan, "Political Islam in Turkey", *Turkish Studies*, 6(1), 2005, 3–19.
7 For sacralization of politics, see Emilio Gentile, *The Sacralization of Politics in Italy* (Cambridge, MA: Harvard University Press, 1996).
8 İsmail Çağlar, " 'Yeni Türkiye'den Eski Medyaya Bakmak", *Sabah*, September 6, 2014.
9 For the concept of "White Turks", see Doğan Gürpınar, *Ulusalcılık*, 170–179; Rıfat Bali, *Tarz-ı Hayat'tan Life Style'a* (İstanbul: İletişim Yayınları, 2002), 324–377.
10 Ali Nur Kutlu, "Beyaz Türklere Mektup", *Yeni Şafak*, April 23, 2014; Ali Nur Kutlu, "Merkez Kim, Çevre Neresi? Anadolu İnsanı mı, Beyaz Türkler mi?" *Yeni Şafak*, April 16, 2014; Özlem Albayrak, "Şehit ve Beyaz Türk'ün Kaynama Noktası", *Yeni Şafak*, October 11, 2008.
11 For the 2013 Gezi riots and their repercussions, see Doğan Gürpınar, *Kültür Savaşları: İslam, Sekülerizm ve Kimlik Siyasetinin Yükselişi*, 199–236; Umut Özkırımlı (ed.), *The Making of a Protest Movement in Turkey* (Basingstoke: Palgrave Macmillan, 2014); Emrah Göker, Vefa Saygın Öğütle (eds.), *Gezi ve Sosyoloji* (İstanbul: Ayrıntı Yayınları, 2014).
12 For the pressure on the media and government's exertion of power over it, see Mustafa Hoş, *Abluka* (İstanbul: Destek Yayınları, 2014); Mustafa Alp Dağıstanlı, *5 Ne? 1 Kim?* (İstanbul: Postacı Yayınevi, 2014).

13 Cemil Ertem, Markar Esayan, *Dünyayı Durduran 60 Gün* (İstanbul: Etkileşim Yayınları, 2013); Nasuhi Güngör, "On Maddede Gezi Saldırısı", *Star*, June 17, 2013; Nasuhi Güngör, "Yeni Türkiye'yi Anlatmak", *Star*, September 12, 2013; Nasuhi Güngör, "Masum Değil Hiçbiri", *Star*, June 15, 2013; Yasin Aktay, "Gezi'deki Komplo ve Sosyoloji", *Yeni Şafak*, June 22, 2013.

14 İsmet Berkan, "İstanbul'da Trafiği Otpor mu İçinden Çıkılmaz Hale Getirdi?" *Hürriyet*, October 12, 2013.

15 At the time of the submission of the final text of this book, the Open Society Institute finally announced closure of its Turkish office and cessation of its activities in Turkey. This came just after the arrest of civil society activists who were charged for "being in contact and service of Soros and Open Society". Erdoğan also blamed Soros by name as behind Gezi protests and pseudo–civil society opposition in the aftermath of the debacles of these arrests. See Kenan Kıran, "Soros'la Kavala'nın Para Trafiği, "*Sabah*, November 26, 2018; "Kavala Ekibine Gezi Operasyonu", *Sabah*, November 17, 2018.

16 "Kod Adı İstanbul İsyanı", *Yeni Şafak*, June 16, 2013; "Nöbeti Alman Medyası Devraldı", *Yeni Şafak*, June 21, 2013; "Sivil Darbe Engellendi", *Yeni Şafak*, June 9, 2013.

17 Willim Engdahl also contributes regularly to the Russian media writing op eds and partaking in TV discussions. www.rt.com/op-ed/authors/william-engdahl/.

18 Quoted in Doğan Gürpınar, *Komplolar Kitabı* (İstanbul: Doğan Kitap, 2014), 250.

19 For the LGBT movement and the politics of LGBT in Turkey, see Aslı Zengin, "Trans-Beyoğlu: Kentsel Dönüşüm, Şehir Hakkı ve Trans Kadınlar", in Ayfer Bartu Candan, Cenk Özbay (eds.), *Yeni İstanbul Çalışmaları* (İstanbul: Metis Yayınları, 2014), 360–375; Sibel Yardımcı, Dikmen Bekmez, "Normativite sınırında İttifak İmkanları: Heterotopya Olarak Queer ve/ya Sakat Bedenler ve Kamusallığı Beden Üzerinden Okumak", Ayfer Bartu Candan, Cenk Özbay (eds.), *Yeni İstanbul Çalışmaları* (İstanbul: Metis Yayınları, 2014), 309–326; Zeynep Tüfekçi, *Twitter and Tear Gas* (London, New Haven: Yale University Press, 2017), 108.

20 For Putin and the sexual politics of Putinism, see Valerie Sperling, *Sex, Politics, and Putin: Political Legitimacy in Russia* (Oxford: Oxford University Press, 2014).

21 "TRT'den Homofobik Eurovision Savunması", *Cumhuriyet*, August 4, 2018.

22 Melih Altınok, "Bu Trump Size Ne'tti Kardeşim", *Sabah*, December 13, 2016; Salih Tuna, "ABD Başkan Adayı: Fetullah'ın Arkasında . . .", *Sabah*, December 13, 2016; Melih Altınok, "Bu Amerikalılar Hepten Çıldırmadı Ya", *Sabah*, July 30, 2016; Hilal Kaplan, "Bir Daha 'Seviyesizlik'ten Bahseden Olursa . . .", *Sabah*, November 7, 2016.

23 "ABD'de Patlak Veren Sübyanılık Dosyası ile Yer Yerinden Oynadı", *Sabah*, November 17, 2016; "Skandalın Adı Pizzagate, Mağdurları: Çocuklar", *Sabah*, November 27, 2 016.

24 Haşmet Babaoğlu, "Ay Naylon Oldu, Sıra Mars'ta mı?" *Sabah*, November 29, 2018; Haşmet Babaoğlu, "Nüfus Korkusu . . . Yalanlar, Şüpheler . . .", *Sabah*, December 14, 2018; Haşmet Babaoğlu, "Hepsi Yalan, Bir Mars mı Gerçek?" *Sabah*, December 11, 2018; Haşmet Babaoğlu, "Ay, Uzay, Dünya", *Sabah*, October 11, 2018; Haşmet Babaoğlu, "Sırada Virus Salgınları mı Var?" *Sabah*, September 29, 2018; Haşmet Babaoğlu, "Bu Hawking O Hawking mi?" *Sabah*, January 26, 2018.

25 See Haşmet Babaoğlu, "Bilim Dedikleri Bilim Değil Sol Dedikleri Beşinci Kol", *Sabah*, April 9, 2018; Haşmet Babaoğlu, Haşmet Babaoğlu, "Hawking Sonrası . . . Bilmediğini Bilmeyen Kültürlüler!!!", *Sabah*, March 22, 2018.

26 See Yasin Aktay, "Darwin ve Evrim İnancı", *Yeni Şafak*, March 16, 2009; Özlem Albayrak, "İdeolojiniz Özenle Jelatinlenir", *Yeni Şafak*, March 14, 2009; "Yobazlık . . . Her Yerde, Herkeste", *Sabah*, June 6, 2009; Yasin Aktay, "İslam Düşüncesinde Ateizm Eleştirileri", *Yeni Şafak*, September 24, 2018.

27 The "Pelican Brief" to this day remains posted on WordPress: https://pelikandosyasi.wordpress.com/ (retrieved August 27, 2018).

28 For three substantial pieces written on the "Pelicans", see Yıldıray Oğur, "Pelikan'ın İnine Doğru", *Türkiye*, May 13, 2016; Yıldıray Oğur, "Benden Selam Olsun Pelikan Bey'ine", *Türkiye*, May 4, 2016; Efe Kerem Sözeri, "Pelikan Derneği: Berat Albarak, Ahmet Davutoğlu'nu Neden Devirdi?" https://medium.com/@efekerem/pelikan-derne%C4%9Fi-berat-albarak-ahmet-davuto%C4%9Flunu-neden-devirdi-5fabad6dc7de.

29 For Davutoğlu's authorized biography, see Gürkan Zengin, *Hoca* (İstanbul: İnkılap Yayınevi, 2010).

30 Zeynep Tüfekçi, *Twitter and Tear Gas* (London, New Haven: Yale University Press, 2017), 223–260.

31 Ilya Yablokov, "Conspiracy Theories as a Russian Public Diplomacy Tool: The Case of Russia Today (RT)", *Politics*, 35(3–4), 301–315; Peter Pomarentsev, Michael Weiss, *The Menace of Unreality: How the Kremlin Weaponizes Information, Culture and Money* (New York: Institute of Russian Studies, 2014); Peter Pomarentsev, Michael Weiss, "Russian Trolls 'spreading discord' Over Vaccine Safety Online", *The Guardian*, www.theguardian.com/society/2018/aug/23/russian-trolls-spread-vaccine-misinformation-on-twitter; Max Seddon, "Documents Show How Russia's Troll Army Hit America", *Buzzfeed*, June 2, 2014, www.buzzfeed.com/maxseddon/ documents-show-how-russias-troll-army-hit-america#2w346ct.

32 Yasin Aktay, "Darbecilerin Kardeşliği", *Yeni Şafak*, July 27, 2013.

33 Ibid; Yasin Aktay, "Mısır'da İflas Eden Batılı Demokrasi", *Yeni Şafak*, July 8, 2013; Yasin Aktay, "Mısır'ı Kim Kazandı, Kim Kaybetti?" *Yeni Şafak*, July 15, 2013; Yasin Aktay, "Adeviye'de Teselli Arayan Şaşkın Darbeci", *Yeni Şafak*, July 22, 2013.

34 Mehmet Metiner, "Türkiye'nin Baltacıları Darbe İstemiyormuş!" *Yeni Şafak*, August 20, 2013.

35 Ali Nur Kutlu, "Bizim Kavgamız", *Yeni Şafak*, December 3, 2014.

36 Yasin Aktay, "Hasan el-Benna ve İhvan Kimliği", *Yeni Şafak*, May 7, 2012. Ayrıca bakınız, Yasin Aktay, "Hasan el-Benna ve İhvan Sempozyumu", *Yeni Şafak*, May 5, 2012.

37 Ali Nur Kutlu, "Merkez Kim, Çevre Neresi? Anadolu İnsanı mı, Beyaz Türkler mi?" *Yeni Şafak*, April 16, 2014.

38 Yasin Doğan, "Rejim mi İhraç Ediyoruz?" *Yeni Şafak*, August 21, 2013.

39 For the "Hamidophilia verging on Hamidomania", see Edhem Eldem, "Sultan Abdülhamid II: Founding Father of the Turkish State", *Journal of the Ottoman and Turkish Studies Association*, 5(2), 2018, 25–46. I thank Nicholas Danforth for bringing this piece to my attention.

40 For the reactions of the Turkish Jewish community in the Jewish weekly *Şalom*, see Marsel Russo, "Yıkılan Tarih", *Şalom*, March 8, 2017; Elif Uğur, "Gerçek Osmanlıcılık Bu Değil", *Şalom*, March 8, 2017.

41 For critical evaluations of the series, see Yıldıray Oğur, "Bu Bölüm Dizide Yok", *Karar*, January 20, 2018; Murat Bardakçı, "Payitaht İstanbul", *Habertürk*, March 1, 2017; Murat Bardakçı, "Ayıptan da Öte Bir İş", *Habertürk*, March 27, 2018.

42 For the relations between Abdülhamid II and the nascent Zionist movement, see Vahdettin Ergin, *Pazarlık* (İstanbul: Yeditepe Yayınevi, 2013); Sezai Balcı, Mustafa Balcıoğlu, *Rotschildler ve Osmanlı İmparatorluğu* (İstanbul: Erguvani Yayınevi, 2017).

43 "Erdoğan Sordu: 'O Diziyi İzliyorsunuz, Değil mi'?" *Türkiye*, December 31, 2017.

44 For the Sykes–Picot treaty, see James Barr, *A Line in the Sand* (New York: Simon & Schuster, 2012).

45 www.hurriyet.com.tr/basbakan-davutoglu-kutul-amareyi-anlamayan-23-nisani-anlayamaz-40096971.

46 For some ruminations over the Sykes–Picot theme, see Akif Emre, "Post-Sykes Picot Modeli mi?" *Yeni Şafak*, October 13, 2015; Yasin Aktay, "Yüz Yıl Sonra Yeni bir Sykes Picot mu?" *Yeni Şafak*, October 24, 2015; Erhan Afyoncu, "İşte Ortadoğu'yu Kan Gölüne Çeviren İki Batılı: Sykes ve Picot", *Sabah*, February 7, 2016.

47 Yıldıray Oğur, "Unuttuğumuzu Unutmanın Hikayesi", *Karar*, February 10, 2018.

48 www.hurriyet.com.tr/basbakan-davutoglu-kutul-amareyi-anlamayan-23-nisani-anlayamaz-40096971.

49 Mustafa Armağan, "Kûtu'l-Amâre Zaferi Neden Unutturuldu?" *Derin Tarih*, (49), April 2016, 3–4.

50 "MEB'in yeni 'Değer'i Cihad", *Cumhuriyet*, January 15, 2017.

51 For the historical populism of the AKP, see Büke Koyuncu, *"Benim Milletim": AK Parti İktidarı, Din ve Ulusal Kimlik* (İstanbul: İletişim Yayınları, 2014), 79–176.

52 "Kûba Camii Buraya Yapılacak", *Sabah*, November 16, 2014.

53 "Kolomb'dan Önce İslamiyet Gitti", *Akşam*, November 17, 2014; Akif Emre, "Amerika'yı Keşfetmenin Bedeli", *Yeni Şafak*, November 18, 2014, www.timeturk.com/tr/makale/nevzat-cicek/amerikan-kitasini-muslumanlar-kesfetti-iste-kanitlari.html#.VGjhyPSUeDo.

54 William Friedrich Dame, *The Muslim Discovery of America* (Books on Demand, 2013), 389–390.

55 Abdurrahman Dilipak, *Coğrafi Keşiflerin İçyüzü* (İstanbul: İnkılab Yayınları, 1984).

56 "'Duşakabinoğulları' İstifa Getirdi", www.diken.com.tr/dusakabinogullari-istifa-getirdi-o-kiyafete-bornoz-diyen-dekan-gorevinden-ayrildi/.

57 "İstanbul'da Fetih Şöleni", *Milliyet*, May 31, 2015.

58 For the YouTube upload of the documentary, see the link www.youtube.com/watch?v=Zqw2eZ1K6Uw.

59 Murat Akan, *Üst Akıl: Derin İktidarın Küresel Efendileri*, (İstanbul: Hayat, 2016).

60 Gilber Achar, *The Arabs and the Holocaust* (New York: Metropolitan Books, 2010).

61 Timothy Snyder, *The Road to Unfreedom* (New York: Tim Duggan Books, 2018), 33–40.

62 Ibid., 30.

63 For the conspiracy theories in Russia, also see Ilya Yablokov, *Fortress Russia: Conspiracy Theories in Post-Soviet Russia* (London: Polity, 2018).

Conclusion

This short book has provided an overview of the conspiracy theories that have abounded in Turkey over one-and-a-half centuries of the historical continuum. It began by emphasizing that unlike the contemporary rise of conspiracy theories in the West, where they were the exclusive preserve of the right wing before they went appallingly mainstream, in Turkey, the conspiratorial mind-set was heavily entrenched within the seed of nationalism that swelled after being planted in the late 19th century. This mental frame stemmed from the fear of foes both within and without, who were imagined as being in close cooperation and collaboration ranging from European imperialist powers to local protestors. The Lausanne Treaty succeeded to terminate the "Eastern Question" and stabilized the region rendering any border change highly unlikely and securing the dawn of the age of nation-states. Yet the mistrust prevailed toward the enemies who were seen as not giving up their ambitions but as concealing them, waiting for the opportune time. The frenzy rising over the trauma of the painful dissolution of the Ottoman Empire was moderated by the transition to democracy and Turkey's alignment with the West in the Cold War.

The end of the Cold War, however, left the Western alliance redundant in the eyes of Western skeptics. This was not a geopolitical proposition but an ideological one, stemming from hostility towards liberal values and historical encounters with imperialism that had sought to destroy Turkey. For many, non-European alternatives (known generically as Euro-Asianism) became viable and desirable, and this stance instigated an anti-Westernist animus that was infatuated with conspiracy theories exposing how the imperialist and Christian West was resolute in its desire to partition Turkey in collaboration with its allies within, continuing the cause of the thousand-year-old Crusades. Domestic conflicts, unrest and tension were interlinked with this imperialist scheming. These conspiratorial themes were in fact borrowed from the late Ottoman and early republican conspiratorial reservoir that had emerged out of the vexation of imperialist aggression until the Eastern Question was resolved in 1923.

Yet in the 2000s, the rise of political Islam prompted and boosted a new and even sharper wave of conspiracy theories and a conspiratorial culture. The Islamist narratives that had long circulated and reigned among the fringe Islamist circles swiftly came to prominence, to the astonishment of those who were not even aware of them. In fact, when the AKP assumed power in 2002, the reformist Islamist movement denounced the Islamist ideological and cultural heritage that explained the world and the course of the 20th century through the machinations of Zionism, Jewry, secretive Freemasonry and the West as hostage to them. The founders of the AKP initially endorsed a progressive liberal worldview seeking membership to European Union against a highly Euroskeptic secular sentiment, amalgamating liberal values with their Islamic proclivities and so were acclaimed by the liberals (and partially by leftists) as a healthy antidote to the Kemalist guard, which had become infatuated with a conspiratorial worldview. Yet in a decade, the purportedly abandoned Islamist conspiratorial drive returned. Erdoğan arbitrarily manipulated this received conspiratorial imagination to consolidate his power and legitimize his moves by articulating a variety of conspiracy theories that often contradicted and rescinded each other. In this regard, contemporary Islamist conspiratorialism is different from the Islamist old school conspiratorial paradigm in terms of its function. The bombastic articulation of conspiracy theories involves a strategy of identifying lethal national threats against which national solidarity is imperative. This permanent state of emergency helps consolidate Erdoğan's core constituency, while also, aiming to criminalize and/or neutralize "patriotic" opponents rendering courses of events as a matter of national security. As long as the audience is ready to buy these conspiracy theories, they seem to remain, whether in Islamist, nationalist or any other mold.

Index

www.ingramcontent.com/pod-product-compliance
Ingram Content Group UK Ltd.
Pitfield, Milton Keynes, MK11 3LW, UK
UKHW020424010325
455677UK00029B/996